RIVER SAFETY
A Floater's Guide

RIVER SAFETY
A Floater's Guide

Stan Bradshaw

Greycliff Publishing Company
Helena, Montana

Printed in the United States of America

10 09 08 07 06 05 04 03 02 01 00   10 9 8 7 6 5 4 3 2 1

COVER DESIGN BY Geoffrey Wyatt, Helena, Montana

TYPESET IN Minion, Minion Display, and Humanst 521 Cn by Geoffrey Wyatt, Helena, Montana

PRINTED BY Advanced Litho, Great Falls, Montana

Library of Congress Cataloging-in-Publication Data

Bradshaw, Stan, 1949–
    River Safety : a floater's guide / Stan Bradshaw
        p. cm.
    Includes bibliographical references and index.
    ISBN 1-890373-08-7 (alk. paper)
    1. White-water canoeing—Safety measures. 2. Rafting (Sports)—Safety measures. 3. Rivers—Recreational use. I. Title.

GV788.B72 2000
797.1'22'0289—dc21   00-022024

Contents

Acknowledgments

A book like this involves drawing on the collective experience of people far wiser than me to properly cover the terrain of river safety. In putting this book together, I have shamelessly borrowed from the good works of people I haven't even met, perhaps chief among those being Charlie Walbridge, who has probably done more than anyone else in this country to bring river safety to the forefront.

In addition, there were plenty of others who directly answered my pleas for advice. Diane and Jim McDermand, longtime paddlers and instructors, worked the manuscript over with a fine-tooth comb. My thanks to Liz Lodman of the Montana Department of Fish, Wildlife and Parks for reviewing the manuscript from the perspective of a water safety officer and providing me valuable guidance. Dave Glenn of the National Outdoor Leadership School had valuable suggestions for the manuscript. John Cederquist of the University of Utah Recreational Program gave me crucial help in identifying important river-running courses that emphasize skills and safety. Mike Johnston, a whitewater guide and an instructor in swiftwater rescue, gave me valuable advice about fine points of paddle rafting and rescue. Thanks to Al Kesselheim for his discerning criticisms (not the least of which was to gently point out how dumb my working title was—hope this one is better).

Every writer needs an editor. Rick Newby deftly mended my assaults on the language. Geoff Wyatt took the bare text and wove it with the photos and illustrations into a coherent whole.

In the more local perspective, my thanks to fellow canoe instructor and doting parent Bruce Newell for his sage advice on paddling with kids. Joan Connole and Scott Brown, of the Base Camp in Helena, by letting me teach canoe classes for the shop, have provided me with a living, breathing testing ground for much of the information in this book.

And finally, most importantly, my thanks to Glenda, my best canoe partner, for her tolerance, keen eye for detail, the illustrations in the book, and her unfailing support.

Introduction

My first float trip, if you could call it that, is conclusive proof that the laws of natural selection are not infallible. It was in spring 1968, during my freshman year at the University of Montana. My pal Greg had a raft, it was a sunny weekday afternoon, the leaves were just starting to bud out on the maples, and the Clark Fork River, which flows right by the university, was running high but clear. What better day for an afternoon float after class? Greg and I gathered up a couple of buddies, a couple of paddles, some old kapok-filled horse-collar life vests (somebody thought we had to have them in the boat even if we didn't wear them), a few beers—and off we went.

Actually, it wasn't much of a raft—one of those rubbery, yellow, thin-skinned toys that passed for a raft in the local discount sporting goods stores—and it wasn't really much of a float. In the testosterone-poisoned muddle that passes for thought in male college freshmen, we had our sights aimed at the culvert pouring the overflow of an irrigation weir back into the river. The culvert was big, maybe five feet in diameter, and its flow dropped in a graceful arc into a pool four feet below the culvert and immediately adjacent to the main current of the Clark Fork. To us, it looked all the world like a water slide. We would come down the weir, line up on the culvert and (with our two paddles) accelerate smartly through, and blast triumphantly into the holding pool. A regular whitewater adventure right there in the middle of town.

Our course plotted, we put in at the top of the weir, about three hundred yards above the culvert. Once on the water, the plan started to come apart pretty quickly. First, there was the steering problem. It's darn hard to control one of those rubber duckies with two paddles—especially when you're sitting in the bottom of the boat, have never paddled a raft, you've had a couple of beers, and no one is navigating. It was as if each of us reverted to some exotic foreign tongue completely unintelligible to anyone else in the raft. Nonetheless, after a hundred yards or so, our paddlers got the boat going in a more-or-less straight line. At least we were headed downstream. And we were undaunted. After all, we would only have to accelerate for ten feet or so through the culvert. No sweat.

Within a couple of minutes we arrived at the culvert. Somehow, we got lined up and managed a couple of good strokes through the culvert. Then things really went to hell. In our assessment of the culvert as water slide, we made a couple of miscalculations (well, more than a couple, actually). First, the plume of water coming out of the culvert, unlike a water slide, had no firm bed to hold us up. Second, there was no way we could propel that raft fast enough to stay with the current speed as we exited the culvert, even if we had known how to paddle. And third, we hadn't calculated the weight factor of the four guys in the boat. Greg and I, weighing in at a strapping 135 and 150 pounds respectively, were on one side. On the other side were Kevin and Tom, weighing in at 195 and 180 pounds. Not exactly a balanced load.

Quicker than my memory could record, we were upside down as we cleared the culvert. And that's how we entered the pool. Spring runoff on the Clark Fork is numbingly cold. For what seemed like hours (but surely was only seconds), my only response was to try and breathe. I was standing and bouncing in only five feet of water, but I couldn't get my breath. When I finally did, I found that my muscles were stiff and wooden. If I had needed to swim, I would have drowned. I looked over at Greg on the other end of the raft. He was blindly pawing at the raft as though to get a purchase. Something was wrong with this picture. Then it hit me. Greg was missing his glasses. When he finally got a grip on the raft, we managed to drag it to shore. Tom and Kevin crawled out on the other bank. For a few minutes, we just sat on shore, trying to get our breath and bearings back.

When we had the energy to assess our damage, it wasn't a pretty picture. While no one had drowned or been seriously injured (there were a couple of nicks and bruises from clambering up on the rocky shore), our equipment had taken a major hit. Greg never did find his glasses, and our four life jackets (conveniently stowed in the middle of the raft where they wouldn't get in our way) were headed toward Idaho, along with our two paddles. The raft, not designed for high-altitude entry into water, had some seam leaks. We stumbled back to our dorm (leaving the raft on shore), got warm showers and dry clothes, and then chased down our lost equipment. Amazingly, besides Greg's glasses, we lost only one paddle and one life jacket.

That night, dry, fed, boozed, and relatively unscathed, in the tradition of youthful adventurers—enthusiastic but not very bright—we reveled in our adventure without a thought as to how it might have turned out.

So what did we do wrong on that maiden voyage? The list of what we did right would be much shorter. But here are the highlights in our little carnival of errors—alcohol, inexperience, unused life jackets (also known as personal flotation devices or PFDs), inadequate equipment, poor (read that as "no") planning, and absolutely no understanding of the limits of our craft or our abilities, So why did we survive our descent through the tube? Dumb luck.

There were many more floats, and at least a few more near misses, before I began to reflect seriously on just how much the beneficiaries of dumb luck we had been. Fortunately for me, over time, I came under the influence of people wiser than myself who were able to teach me a thing or two about commonsense river safety.

Nonetheless, it took what seemed to me to be a disastrous year of river accidents for me to recognize that more needed to be said about river safety.

The summer of 1996 will stand in my memory as a benchmark for river accidents in Montana. Over the course of several weeks it seemed as though there was a river fatality at every turn—a baby drowned in the Clark Fork, a rafter drowned on the Gallatin, another rafter on the Madison, an angler in a driftboat on the Big Hole . . . The body count grew at an alarming rate that year.

What was most striking about these accidents was that many of them weren't in big, technical, difficult whitewater. And most disquieting was that almost all of them involved lapses of judgment that were totally avoidable by adherence to a few simple rules of behavior. When I began to reflect on other river fatalities over the last few years, it seemed obvious that the vast majority of those deaths resulted from the violation of the most basic rules of river safety.

Obvious to me, anyway. Over years of instructor certification courses with the American Canoe Association, and in the course of teaching canoeing on waters ranging from the local pond to whitewater on the Blackfoot River, I'd had the basic tenets of river safety drilled into me. Those lessons have been reinforced over the years by the literature on river safety, especially the chilling, graphic, and completely riveting accounts of river accidents in the *River Safety Newsletter* series by Charlie Walbridge for the American Canoe Association. So why were so many people dying so needlessly?

Part of the answer is fairly simple. Most people who float rivers— whether in a canoe, raft, driftboat, or kayak—haven't had any training in river safety. I know dozens of floaters who have floated for years without serious consequence—and some of them have even developed considerable skill in their craft—who don't know the first thing about how to reduce the odds of a serious or fatal accident on the river. At least a few of those floaters, like me in my youth, have survived their own ignorance and bad judgment by nothing more than the intervention of dumb luck. Ironically, these boaters may represent the norm in our river-running tradition. And as more and more people flock to our rivers, more of us are dying.

There is a significant body of good literature on river safety and river rescue already in existence. The bibliography in the back of this book offers a sampling of some of the best of it. But most of it, as good as it is, focuses on the experienced boater who already has some grounding in, or at least appreciation of, river safety and river rescue. This book is an attempt to reach the vast majority of boaters who have not been exposed to any sort of organized river safety training.

My primary objective is to give boaters, especially entry-level boaters, some basic tools to avoid becoming an accident statistic— basic principles of navigation, the most common causes of river fatalities, objective river hazards and how to avoid them, and some basic skills of self- and assisted rescue.

In preparation for this book, I combed accident report files at the Montana Department of Fish, Wildlife, and Parks, reviewing more than fifty accidents occuring over a dozen years. Rather than simply discussing safety issues in the abstract, I have couched much of the discussion in the context of these river accidents. In doing this, I am shamelessly borrowing from the example of Charlie Walbridge's excellent *River Safety Newsletter* series. There is nothing quite so compelling as these accounts of river accidents and what went wrong. I propose to take the idea a step further, however, and embellish the accounts with more explanation of the precepts of river safety and how to apply them. In a few cases, I have included accounts of lake accidents that vividly illustrate the violation of some basic safety rule that can apply equally to rivers.

These accounts are not meant to frighten anyone away from the river. But if they shake your complacency or cause you discomfort in recollecting the bullets you may have dodged while breaking basic rules, then so much the better.

If these accounts of accidents make you want to become a more skilled river runner and to pursue river safety training on a more formal level, then I have achieved my purpose. Make no mistake. This book is not a substitute for a class of instruction in canoeing, rafting, kayaking, or river rescue. There are many good courses throughout the country on these topics. If you haven't taken a class already, find one and take it. It is money well spent. Especially if it keeps you alive.

So read the book, think about its lessons, and then go run a river and have some fun. In fact, have a lot of fun. After all, that's what messing around on rivers is supposed to be about. But be careful out there.

River Terminology
A Glossary

A glossary usually appears at the back of a book. That's never made much sense to me. I would rather see the definitions at the front, where I can peruse them in the normal progression of reading the book. Most, but not all, of the terms in this glossary appear elsewhere in the book. If not, you may hear it on the river. Maybe if you read it here first, you'll have some context for it elsewhere. Peruse the following definitions of common river terms now—it's not all that long a list—and maybe you won't have to keep looking for the "glossary" every time you come to a river term in the book.

Broach. A boat broaches when the current pushes it sideways into an obstacle that stops it dead in the river. In many cases, the broach is immediately followed by the current pulling the upstream side of the boat under, wrapping the boat around the obstacle. Wrapping is bad. To avoid wrapping, lean the boat or move the people toward the obstacle before you broach and try to keep the upstream side from getting pulled under. See "high side."

Cubic feet per second (cfs). The most common description of the volume of a river's flow. A cfs is one cubic foot of water passing a fixed point in one second. A cfs equals 448 gallons per minute. For the mathematically impaired, ten thousand cfs is a lot of water.

Downstream V. Downstream Vs are the surface signs of current running through obstacles or between shallows. The downstream V marks the deeper water. As a rule of thumb, downstream Vs point to the channel, whereas upstream Vs point to rocks and obstacles. See "Tongue" below.

Eddy. The place in a river immediately downstream of an obstacle, such as a rock or an outcrop of land, into which the current flows from below the obstacle, forming a pocket of upstream current.

Eddy line. The interface formed between the prevailing downstream current and the upstream current of an eddy. When the opposing currents are strong enough, the interface may actually create a bulge in the surface that can be harder to get across. That bulge is an eddy "fence."

Eddy turns and peel-outs. The technique of turning your craft out of (eddy turn) or into (peel out) the prevailing downstream current, using opposing current directions to assist the turn.

Ferrying. Using boat angle and upstream momentum to move laterally across a current. It is possible to ferry with the front of the boat facing downstream (back ferry) or, in some boats, with the front of the boat facing upstream (front ferry).

Gradient. The steepness of a river's descent. Usually measured in feet per mile (fpm).

High side. Believe it or not, this is a verb. You "high side" a boat when you—and anyone else in the boat with you—move to one side of the boat to avoid having the boat flip or, in some instances, to avoid being pulled through a strainer.

Hole. A river feature created by water flowing over and around an obstacle at a near-vertical gradient, causing the current to circulate back up to the obstacle.

Hydraulic. A really bad hole. The hole below a low-head dam is a hydraulic. Likewise, you'll see them below ledges or steep pourovers.

Ledge. A ledge occurs when a riverbed undergoes a sudden elevation drop that extends across all or part of the river.

Low-head dam. A short dam over which the river flows, creating a river-wide hole. Also known as a "drowning machine."

Personal flotation device (PFD). Also known as "life vest" or "life jacket." A PFD is a buoyant device to keep a person afloat in the water. Buy a good one. Wear it.

Pillow. An upwelling of water on the upstream side of a rock or bank which, when big enough, can deflect a boat around the obstacle.

Pourover. An obstacle close to the surface with a steep drop on the downstream side, often forming a hole. A pourover can be hard to read from upstream. It may be a nice surfing wave, or it may be a hole. Avoid going over it if you don't know which it is.

River left/river right. Describing relative position on the river *as you look downstream*. Use the downstream frame of reference even if you are looking upstream as you speak. Make sure that everyone in your group is talking the same language on this one. Confusion can be disastrous.

Setting. Another term for a back ferry to move a boat laterally. Instead of "Back ferry right," you may hear "Set right." An old term that isn't much used any more, except by hidebound old canoeists.

Stoppers. These are waves in which the crest curls back upstream on itself. Good for flipping or filling boats. For advanced boaters, they can be great surfing waves.

Strainer. An obstacle, often a fallen tree or logjam, that rests in the water with part of its structure under the surface. The current will pull things (e.g. boats, bodies) down and through whatever subsurface appendages are down there, "straining" them out of the flow.

Surfing. A river maneuver in which the boat gets on the upstream face of a wave and stays there, held by gravity on the upstream face and the current going under the boat. On really big water, even rafts surf.

Sweeper. A riverside feature, often a tree, that has fallen out over the current with branches or other appendages extending down toward (or even to) the water. If you attempt to pass through a sweeper, those appendages can "sweep" you out of your boat. A big enough sweeper may also have some characteristics of a strainer.

Throw bag/throw rope. A rope stuffed in a bag for throwing to a swimmer in need of rescue.

Tongue. Another term for "downstream V"; see above.

Undercut rocks or bank. Rocks or banks in which the upstream face of the rock slopes downstream under the surface. Current flows into these and downward in much the same way current goes through a strainer. Hint—current going into an undercut rock or bank may not form a pillow on the upstream side because there is nothing immediately under the surface to deflect the water upstream.

Weir. Another name for a dam. Often you may hear this term in reference to an irrigation diversion.

Chapter One
Five Deadly Mistakes

Running rivers carries some inherent risk, no matter how carefully you prepare. Throughout the annals of accidents in the United States, there are accounts of highly competent paddlers who, having taken all possible precautions, challenged waters at the limits of their abilities and died. Increasingly, those accidents are the ones that get most of the press. Nonetheless, the vast majority of fatal river accidents involve violations of some simple precepts of common sense that were entirely within the power of the victim to avoid.

The American Canoe Association has gone to considerable effort over the course of many years to track the causes of fatal boating accidents. Following are their findings of the Top Five Causes:

1. The victims failed to wear personal flotation devices (life jackets).
2. The water or the weather was cold.
3. The victims were inexperienced.
4. Alcohol or drugs were contributing factors.
5. The victims were non-swimmers.

The following discussion focuses on incidents in which accidents resulted from one, or a combination, of these five causes. Often, where you find one of these problems, you find more. While I will emphasize one cause in each incident, I will note the other factors that contributed to the accident or the death.

The First Deadly Mistake
Failure to Wear Personal Flotation Devices

After inexperience, the failure to wear a personal flotation device (PFD) is the most common contributor to boating fatalities. Of the thirty-eight fatal Montana boating accidents surveyed in preparation for this book, eleven involved either failure to wear a PFD or wearing an ill-fitting PFD. My correspondence indicates that the figures are similar around the country.

Drowning on the Flathead River

On September 14, 1995, Jerry, Staci, Melanie, and Martha put in at Bresentine Bar of the Flathead River, intending to float to Spruce Park Campground. All four were in a seventeen-foot canoe. Although there were four PFDs in the boat, only two of the four wore them. At the confluence of two channels, the heavily loaded canoe got caught in a whirlpool and flipped. Jerry was not wearing his PFD. After surfacing and calling for help, he disappeared. One of the women, after making it to shore, ran to a phone to call for assistance.

Rescue personnel arrived within fifteen minutes and brought Jerry to shore, where they administered CPR until an ambulance arrived. They couldn't revive him.

The weather on September 14 was mild. It was clear and warm (75 degrees F), and the wind was calm. The water temperature was 54 degrees. The river was relatively calm in this stretch, except for some squirrelly hydraulics.

Jerry was thirty-nine years old, and he knew how to swim.

Primary Factors Contributing to the Accident:

1. Overloading. Four adults (an aggregate weight of nearly six hundred pounds in this case) in a seventeen-foot canoe would severely impede the ability to maneuver and stabilize the boat in difficult currents. While a canoe properly loaded with gear might easily weigh that much and still be stable, four adults—all likely to move around, at least some, in the canoe—are too much. With that much loose, shifting weight in the boat, the margin for error declines significantly.

2. Inexperience. While the operator of the boat (the accident report didn't say who the "operator" was) apparently had more than five hundred hours of experience, none of the party had any formal training in handling their canoe. A basic course likely would have given them the skills to handle the converging currents and would have taught them not to overload the canoe.

3. Operator inattention. The convergence of two currents on a river typically produces disruptions in the flow that, if not anticipated, can capsize a canoe. Boaters have to constantly look ahead and anticipate hazards. See Chapter Three, Navigation.

Primary Factor Contributing to the Fatality:

Failure to wear a PFD. In this case, the lack of a PFD was literally the difference between life and death. The two women who wore their PFDs survived, as did the woman who did not wear her PFD. She was lucky.

Drift Boat Capsizes on the Big Hole

The Big Hole is a popular fishing river, especially in June during the runoff, and many anglers use drift boats with anchors.

On June 23, 1996, a drift boat carrying four anglers inadvertently dropped its anchor into swift water and capsized when the anchor caught on the bottom. The anchor rope had a knot in the end so the operator was unable to completely release the anchor when it snagged bottom.

There were PFDs in the boat, but they were inaccessible and nobody was wearing one. Three of the four anglers made it to shore. The fourth drowned.

On June 23, the air temperature was approximately 65 degrees F, and the winds were calm. The reach in which the accident occurred contained small waves. The water temperature, however, was 45 degrees F, which is extremely cold. The shock of immersion in water that cold can make swimming difficult.

Primary Factor Contributing to the Accident:

Equipment failure and inadequate safety precautions. Throughout the West, anchors are popular on hard-sided drift boats, allowing anglers to stop and fish specific reaches of the river or to moor the boat on shore during a break from floating. In fast, rough current, however, anchors can be dangerous. Further, one investigator noted that the anchor rope had a knot in it that precluded the rope from simply paying out of the boat and eventually releasing the boat before it sank completely. They would have lost their anchor, but saved their boat and the people in it. A fair trade-off.

On a river trip characterized by heavy currents and fast water, the safest thing you can do is to leave the anchor at home. It may not be quite as convenient to do without it, but as this group learned, having it may not be worth the risk. If you have to have an anchor, make sure that the anchor line can pay out until it leaves the boat. Also, keep a sharp knife close at hand (either on your life vest or attached to the boat close to the anchor line), so that you can cut the anchor line if necessary.

Primary Factors Contributing to the Fatality:

1. Failure to wear a PFD. While three of the four people in this boat made it to shore, the chances of the victim surviving to reach shore would have been much higher had she worn a properly fitting PFD.

2. Cold water. A water temperature of 45 degrees is so cold that, for many people, the shock of immersion is paralyzing. Breathing can be difficult, and strength and coordination quickly disappear. If immersed long enough, you can simply die of hypothermia, even with a PFD. Without the PFD, your chances of survival decline significantly. Proper clothing might have increased the victim's chance of survival.

A Calm-Water Drowning on the Missouri River

On July 5, 1994, Bob and Jack were fishing from a drift boat about a mile south of Craig. While trading places in the boat, Jack tripped and fell, hitting his head and falling out of the boat. He was not wearing a life jacket. Immediately after falling in, he started swimming away from the boat toward the middle of the river. Before Bob could get to him, he had drowned.

On the day in question, the air temperature was 75 degrees at approximately 1:00 p.m. when the accident occurred. The Missouri in this stretch is calm and relatively slow and poses no structural hazards to swimming. One observer suggested, however, that the water temperature may have been in the mid-40s. Jack was in his early seventies.

Primary Factor Contributing to the Accident:
Simple carelessness. Instead of pulling the boat over and getting out, Jack and Bob opted to do a moving exchange. This sort of moving exchange is pretty common on slow-moving waters like the Missouri. Rather than wasting time pulling over, it seems like a simple enough trick to just make a mid-river switch. Nine times out of ten it goes off without a hitch. That tenth time can be a killer.

Primary Factor Contributing to the Fatality:
Failure to wear a PFD. In this case, in a relatively calm current, a life jacket certainly would have increased Jack's chance for survival. Given a head injury, his failure to wear a PFD may have sealed his fate.

This stretch of the Missouri appears to be innocuous. Fishermen, canoeists, rafters, and even inner tubers flock to the river in good weather (on a warm weekend, it can be a veritable zoo), usually without serious mishap. As illustrated here, even the most innocuous water can be dangerous. Don't take the rivers you float for granted. Wear your PFD.

Coast Guard–Approved PFDs—
A Comparative Look at What's Available

The United States Coast Guard has set the design standards for personal flotation devices. The Coast Guard classifies PFDs as five different types, as follows:

Type I PFD. This is for rough, open water. It is the most buoyant of all PFDs and will automatically turn your face up in the water, even if you are unconscious. The disadvantage is that it is quite bulky and not all that comfortable to wear if you are really active in the boat.

Type II PFD. This is commonly (but not necessarily fondly) known as the horse collar. It is for relatively calm inland water where the chance for a fast rescue is fairly good. The advantage is that it will float you high and will turn you face-up if you are unconscious. The downside with this PFD is that it is uncomfortable (especially around the top of the neck) and it provides none of the insulation value that other PFDs commonly do. Beyond some specific children's sizes, one size in the horse collar pretty much fits all. You can pick up some version of this one at just about any discount sporting goods store. This PFD is so uncomfortable that most people are tempted to take it off. Once it's off, it's awkward to get back on so, in a crisis, it is effectively useless to you. If you plan on doing anything more than lily dipping around the local pond, skip this one and buy something you will wear.

Type III PFD. This is the PFD that you will most likely see on the river. It's designed to be comfortable while paddling or fishing. Type IIIs allow you to get a really close fit. One disadvantage is that, unlike Types I and II, the Type III PFD won't float you face-up automatically. It is the choice of most serious floaters because, when properly fitted, it will give you good buoyancy while still allowing you freedom to paddle comfortably.

Type IV PFD. These are the throwable devices. They encompass everything from life-saving rings to buoyant cushions. If your boat is a canoe or kayak or less than sixteen feet long, the law does not require you to carry these in the boat. It's not a bad idea to carry one in any event.

Type V PFD. These are inflatable devices, usually inflated by a CO_2 cartridge.

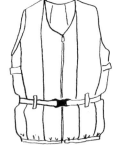

Make sure you choose the PFD most suitable for your activity. If you are running rivers, some variation of the Type III will be your best choice.

Type I

Type III

Type II

Type IV

Child Overboard in Alberton Gorge

On July 6, 1996, three adults and three children (aged two, three, and five) launched a ten-foot raft on the Clark Fork River upstream from the head of Alberton Gorge, a popular and challenging whitewater stretch. The adults in the party were inexperienced boaters. While the details of this accident are sketchy, it appears that not everyone was wearing a PFD. Apparently, the victim, two-year-old Ethan, was wearing an adult-size PFD. At Rest Stop Rapid, the first rapid at the head of the gorge, the raft flipped. Ethan fell out of the raft and was not seen again. Several days of searching failed to turn up either Ethan or his life jacket.

On the day in question, the weather was clear and the air temperature was 80-plus degrees F. The river, however, which is challenging at any water level, was unusually high for early July because of a heavy snowpack.

Primary Factors Contributing to the Accident:

1. Inexperience. Alberton Gorge, with rapids ranging from big class II to class IV is water only for expert boaters. The adults in charge of this raft were much too inexperienced to successfully navigate this reach of the river. That they brought children on the edge of infancy and did not have everyone properly fitted in PFDs is indication enough of just how inexperienced they were. (For an explanation of the classification system for whitewater, see Chapter Two, Reading the Water.)

2. Dangerous conditions. Even though Rest Stop Rapid is challenging at low flows, it was even more hazardous than normal for early July because of the heavy runoff. The difficulty of a river can vary greatly depending on the flow level.

Primary Factor Contributing to the Fatality:

Improper fit of PFD. A PFD that doesn't fit properly may still allow you to drown. It will just take a little longer. While the lack of proper fit was extreme in this example, the bad fit can be much more subtle and still lead to drowning.

PFDs for Children

All too often, perfectly loving, caring parents outfit their kids with whatever happens to be handy in the way of PFDs. As illustrated by the previous example, the results of this approach can be disastrous. Of all the pieces of equipment in boating, your kid's PFD is not the place to scrimp. Get a good quality PFD that fits. If your child is under twelve, get one with leg loops that keep the jacket from riding up and get one that will keep your child face-up.

A properly designed PFD for an infant or small child will include a crotch strap, flotation collar, and a grab loop.

Keeping your Kids Safe On the River

Show your kids a good, safe time afloat. Here are some tips for keeping boating fun—and safe— for your kids.

1. Kids trust adults not to put them in danger. So don't. Make sure you can handle the craft and the water you will be on (this applies with or without your kids). Know your limits and stay well within them.

2. Make sure your kids learn how to swim and become comfortable in the water.

3. Dress for success. Brings lots of extra clothes for kids and extra footwear in a waterproof bag. Your kids will likely get soaked, and there is a good chance they'll lose at least one shoe from every pair you bring.

4. Make sure you always have at least one adult in the boat with them.

5. Much of your kids' and your own water-borne crabby behavior is due to hunger and dehydration. Keep your kids well fed and well hydrated on the river.

6. Put your kids in comfortable, well-fitting life jackets, and make sure they wear them. Make sure you always wear yours. Adults without life jackets set poor examples and will be less able to help their kids if the boat capsizes.

7. Leave your kids home on the really cold-water, cold-weather days.

8. Keep short days on the water when there are kids along, and remember that what's fun for adults may not be so fun for kids.

Bruce Dodges a Bullet on the Sun River

The upper reaches of the Sun River below Gibson Dam pour through a narrow chute, accelerating the flow and making it extremely turbulent. In 1989, during a canoe-instructor training course, Bruce and Diane tipped over while practicing eddy turns. The swift current quickly swept them downstream. Bruce, wearing a wet suit and high-quality PFD, found himself in momentary trouble. Here's what happened, in his words:

> When I first hit the water, my first thought was "Wow, it's cold" (this was late May). I knew I had to get out of the water fast, so I let go of the boat and started kicking for shore. I quickly realized that my vest was not keeping my head completely out of water. The water line was right at my lips, and each time I drew a breath, I took in water. For a few seconds, I thought I was going to drown. Once I got through the panic of that thought, I started kicking harder, breathing more carefully, and managed to get to shore. It was a struggle. The problem? My vest was too big and rode up on my body so it wouldn't float my mouth above water. I went out the next week and bought a new vest.

Getting the Proper Fit on Your PFD

When buying PFDs, people tend to err towards a jacket that is loose fitting. Typically the rationale is comfort. "If it's too tight, it will chafe and pinch," they'll say. Or "if it's too tight, I can't breathe." While both of these can be true, it is possible to get a snug-fitting, comfortable PFD.

Wearing a loose PFD can be fatal. A loose-fitting PFD may float you, but likely not high enough to keep your mouth and nose above water. As a result of wearing a loose-fitting PFD, you stand a good chance of drowning with most of your head above water—a unique, and altogether unpleasant, experience.

A loose-fitting PFD may be as bad as no PFD at all if it doesn't float you high enough to keep your nose and mouth above the water.

It's simple to get a PFD that fits well. Here's how you do it:

1. Put on the PFD you want to buy, zip it up, buckle the belt, and pull the adjustment straps until they are snug (ideally, the PFD should have a range of adjustability so that you can get a snug, but comfortable fit over a range of clothing, from a T-shirt to a pile sweater to a parka or raincoat). Try some paddling motions to make sure the PFD doesn't chafe or

impair your range of motion.

2. You'll need another person for this part—kneel or sit, and with your arms raised over your head, ask a shop employee, friend, or significant other to lift the PFD by the shoulder straps as high as it will go. If the neck of the PFD goes up to your chin, it's too large. Try another one. If it completely pulls off your body, take that as a hint; try one a couple of sizes smaller or get a bigger body.

This PFD is too big for the wearer, riding up so that it won't keep her head above water, or worse, coming completely off if she tries to actively swim.

This PFD fits properly, and will keep her afloat even if she gets her arms above her head. Remember to use the adjustment straps to get a snug fit.

Care and Feeding of Your PFD

A decent PFD (not those five-dollar horse collars at the discount store) can cost anywhere from thirty-five dollars to well over one hundred dollars. Once you have shelled out your hard-earned cash for the right PFD, treat it like your best friend. It may be just that when you least expect it. A few emphatic "don'ts" to ensure your PFD a long and happy life:

1. Don't use your PFD as a pillow, cushion, or lunchtime lounge chair. The flotation in virtually all modern PFDs is closed-cell foam, which compresses over time. The repeated crushing of your PFD will lessen its buoyancy. If you need something to sit on, buy a Crazy Creek chair. They are cheaper and way more comfortable.

2. Don't leave your PFD lying around for extended periods (days to weeks) in the sun, wind, rain, and other elements. While PFDs are supposed to get wet and will hold up to a great deal of punishment, the foam is susceptible to ultraviolet (UV) damage over time. UV damage will harden the foam and make it less buoyant. Likewise, the material covering the foam, usually some kind of nylon, will eventually rot. UV rays accelerate that process. Drying and storing your PFD out of the elements will extend its life considerably.

3. When packing your gear, don't put your PFD at the bottom of the pile and don't put heavy stuff on top of it. (Compression again. See #1 above.)

Cardinal Rules on PFDs

1. Wear your PFD.
2. Make sure your PFD fits.
3. Wear your PFD.
4. Don't sit on your PFD—take care of your PFD.
5. Wear your PFD, and in case you missed it:
6. Wear your PFD.

About Those Buoyancy Ratings

On the label of every PFD (if you read it closely enough), you'll find language that reads, "Buoyant material provides a minimum buoyant force of 15 pounds, 8 ounces" or something to that effect. The weight will vary according to the amount of flotation a jacket provides. The first impulse is to look at this figure in disbelief. Fifteen pounds? No way. Way. Buoyancy correlates to the effective weight of a human when in water. Most of us weigh between ten and fifteen pounds in the water. Talk about your quick weight-loss program.

Some PFDs have as much as twenty-nine pounds of flotation. Why so much? It floats you higher.

The Second Deadly Mistake
Not Preparing for Cold Water and Cold Weather

The most obvious result of exposure to cold water and cold weather is hypothermia. Perhaps just as disabling, however, is the immediate effect from immersion in cold water. Often, when water is extremely cold (below 50 degrees F), your first problem may simply be to breathe. It isn't that you forget to breathe; it's more a matter of your lungs not doing what you will them to do—a little like being hit in the solar plexus. Of course, if you're struggling to breathe, you are probably not attending to other important things, like swimming or getting to shore. Within an unbelievably short time, your ability to do much of anything disappears as your muscles (especially those in your extremities) cease to function. Shortly after that, if you're still alive, you slip further into the hypothermia rut, and soon you're dead from hypothermia or drowning, brought on by your inability to do anything to save yourself. It's a vicious cycle. You can't swim because it's too cold, but if you don't swim, you die.

One obvious precaution is to not paddle in either cold water or cold weather. For those of us in the northern latitudes, that would preclude paddling most of the year, since cool weather (and that's all it really takes) can happen in any month. Even worse, in many areas, the optimum water conditions occur in the spring, when weather and water are likely to be cold. So, many of us are going to paddle in the spring, the obvious risks notwithstanding.

Hypothermia Claims a Life on the North Fork of the Flathead

In late May 1995, Rhoda, Cindy, and Melody launched a rented raft at the Ford Creek access site on the North Fork of the Flathead River. None of the three had much experience running rivers. In fact, it was the first time they had attempted a float trip on their own. While the air temperature was relatively mild for springtime in northern Montana (about 65 degrees F during the day), the water was high and cold (approximately 50 degrees F).

Not long after putting in, they capsized the raft. All three made it back into the raft. Rhoda was showing signs of hypothermia, and Cindy and Melody had to help her get back into the raft. The three capsized at least two more times and again had to swim. Rhoda was becoming increasingly hypothermic. The raft then hit a logjam. Cindy and Melody flushed through and made their way to an island, but Rhoda—who had tied herself to the raft—was caught in the logjam. About an hour after landing on the island, Cindy and Melody saw the raft go by with Rhoda's body still tied to it. Searchers rescued Cindy and Melody the next day. Both were hypothermic.

Rhoda was in her late thirties, was a strong swimmer, and wore a life jacket and several layers of clothing. She had, however, tied herself to the raft. And after the raft capsized the first time, the group did not stop to warm up.

A road paralleled the reach in which the three were floating The air temperature was 65 degrees and the water temperature was 50 degrees.

Primary Factor Contributing to the Accident:

Inexperience. Collectively, the women in this raft had less than twenty hours of floating experience. The North Fork, even at low water, is notorious for its logjams. At high water, it can be a technically demanding and, at times, hazardous river. This group simply did not have the experience to run the North Fork.

Perhaps because of inexperience, there seemed to be no one person in charge of devising a plan or making decisions for the group on the river. While the accident report did not specifically address this point, the circumstances suggest that the group had made no provision for dealing with an upset or accident. See Chapter Five, Trip Organization and River Communication.

Primary Factors Contributing to the Fatality:

1. Hypothermia. While Rhoda appeared to wear proper clothing for cold weather, it was not sufficient to protect her from the effects of cold water. Floating on cold water, where the possibility of immersion exists, requires more than simply layering your clothes. It requires specialized garb, such as a wet suit or a dry suit.

In this case, a second problem was the failure of the group to get off the river and dry out and warm up. While the effects of hypothermia can be abrupt in a cold-water situation, the recovery can be nearly as fast if you get out of the water and warm up. Because the group apparently opted to continue, the effects of hypothermia progressed to more severe stages.

In this case, when Rhoda showed signs of hypothermia even before the last accident, the group priority should have been to get off the river and warm up. After your first upset, it is wise to pull out, warm up, and regroup.

2. Entrapment. Apparently, Rhoda tied herself to the raft (with a carabiner in the back of her life jacket). This likely sealed her fate when the raft hit the logjam. The primary pull of water going through a sweeper is down and under the sweeper (see Chapter 2, Reading the Water). Because she was attached to the raft, Rhoda didn't stand a chance of surviving the sweeper.

One of the most dangerous symptoms of hypothermia is impaired judgment. In this case, the victim became hypothermic relatively early in the float. By the time of the final accident, she was likely not thinking clearly, as suggested by the fact that she tied herself to the raft. *Never tie yourself into your boat.*

The Signs and Symptoms of Hypothermia

As the severity of hypothermia increases, its symptoms will appear in the following order:

1. **Intense shivering,**
2. **Difficulty performing complex tasks,**
3. **Violent shivering,**
4. **Difficulty speaking, sluggishness, forgetfulness,**
5. **Stiff muscles, clumsiness,**
6 **Cessation of shivering,**
7. **Disorientation, irrationality, or apathy,**
8. **Unconsciousness, and finally,**
9. **Cardiac and respiratory failure.**

Dressing and Eating to Prevent Hypothermia

Hypothermia is simply the loss of heat from the body's core. To generate heat, the body needs fuel—food and drink. And it needs shelter (clothing) to maintain the heat that it generates.

Eating and Drinking to Avoid Hypothermia

To avoid hypothermia, the basic rule of thumb for eating and drinking is simply to carry food and fluids with you on the boat and use them constantly.

Instead of following the age-old American eating pattern of three squares a day, graze. Eat and drink moderate amounts all day long. Every half-hour or so, eat something and drink some fluids. Do it even if you don't feel hungry or thirsty. This is a good habit in warm or cold weather.

Why fluids? Dehydration will exacerbate the conditions that lead to hypothermia. Keeping yourself well hydrated will slow the onset of hypothermia.

For food, you want easily digestible, high-calorie foods. Concentrate on carbohydrates—sugars (such as hard candy), fresh and dried fruit, breads, and other starchy foods. On the water, go light on proteins such as meat, milk, cereals (wheat and oats), peas, and beans. Proteins are harder to digest and therefore harder for the body to metabolize.

Whatever you decide to take on the river with you, make sure it is something you like. If you don't like it, you won't eat it. Also, make sure it is in an accessible waterproof container. If you have to unload half your boat each time you want to snack, you won't snack.

Some favorite foods include gorp (my recipe includes M&Ms, raisins, and peanuts—stuff I like to eat—it's the one time I can eat chocolate and feel self-righteous about it), granola, dried fruit, nuts, hard candy, and dried soups. Take along a little backpack stove and a small pan or metal cup—it's really tough to heat water in a plastic cup . . .

Dressing for Hypothermia

Because hypothermia can strike in almost any season in the United States, you should carry enough clothing with you on the boat to adapt to changes in the weather and so that you can change into dry clothes in case of a dunking.

There are a number of specialized paddling clothes now available on the market that are quite effective in combating hypothermia. If you are intent on cool-weather paddling, they are well worth the investment.

The two most important pieces of clothing are dry suits and wet suits.

Dry suits come in two styles: (1) a full-body, one-piece suit, and (2) a two-piece suit with separate top and bottom. They are constructed of heavy-duty coated nylon or more-expensive breathable fabrics with latex gaskets at the neck, wrists, and ankles and a waterproof zipper. When worn over a layer of synthetic long underwear or fleece tops and bottoms, a dry suit is the most effective protection you can have against cold-water immersion. While it will not keep you toasty in cold water, it will keep you warm enough to allow you to breathe and function. Do not be misled by the name "dry suit," however. Between your natural condensation and sweat, dry suits can be downright clammy—a small price to pay for the protection they provide. Another disadvantage of a dry suit is that, on a warm day, you cook. It's a little like having your own portable sauna that follows you everywhere, even when you'd rather not sauna.

Wet suits, made of neoprene rubber and coated with nylon, fit your body snugly and trap and warm a layer of moisture next to your skin. If you capsize while wearing a wet suit, you will stay considerably warmer than you would in street clothes. However, it will not keep you as warm as a dry suit. One advantage is that, unlike a dry suit, a wet suit can be at least moderately comfortable on a warm day. On the downside, the snug fit can make your wet suit uncomfortable over the course of a long day. Another downside is that a wet suit's neoprene can get positively aromatic after a long day or so on the river. Coming across a group of river runners who have been in their wet suits for several days will pretty well put you off your feed for several hours—unless, of course, you too are wet suited. Not the most pleasant side effect, but again a small price to pay for staying warm and alive.

Either a wet suit or a dry suit can entail the expenditure of considerable sums of money. If you are simply an occasional river runner, they may not be worth the investment. In that case, you may find enough clothes in your existing wardrobe to allow you to survive, especially if you already do a number of other outdoor activities. If you're serious about wanting to paddle in the shoulder seasons (spring and fall), however, get either a wet or a dry suit.

Layering. The secret to dressing to prevent hypothermia is to dress in layers. With the proper layers, you can adjust your clothing to provide optimal comfort. The standard layer sequence on a cool day includes the following:

Long underwear—for both the legs and the torso. In wool or synthetic material. Avoid cotton; cotton kills. This may seem like a bit of hyperbole on a hot day when a cotton shirt soaked in water may be the most invigorating thing you can wear. But for the same reason that wet cotton on a hot day feels so good, it can kill you on a cool day—by accelerating evaporative cooling and hastening the effects of hypothermia.

An absorbent layer—for the torso. Appropriate especially on cold days. This layer should include wool or synthetic fleece.

An insulating layer—for the torso. A heavy fleece layer or coat with synthetic fill. Do not wear down. Down is worthless when wet.

A wind- and waterproof layer—for both the legs and the torso. This can be made of coated nylon or any of several breathable, waterproof fabrics.

A warm hat—for the head. This may be as important as anything else you wear. Your head is like a thermostat. On a cool to cold day, you can lose from 50 to 75 percent of your body heat through your head. There are numerous synthetic hats that will keep you warm and will dry quickly when wrung out. My favorite is a fleece-lined Gore-Tex hat with a strap that attaches under my chin. Friends tell me I look like a total dork in it (although they say that about most of my fashion statements), but it has been a lifesaver more than once on the river. It wicks the sweat off my head and keeps me warm.

If you capsize, proper layering can be a passable substitute for a dry suit. A few years back on an Easter Sunday trip down the Blackfoot River in western Montana, my canoe partner and I leaned the wrong way peeling out of an eddy and swam. The water temperature was probably in the high-40s, low-50s. I had loaned her my dry suit (certain, of course, that I wouldn't be swimming), and lacking a wet suit, I'd layered according to the formula above, with a coated-nylon paddle jacket and pants. We both got to shore quickly and got back in the boat. While I wasn't dry—water had come in through the elastic cuffs and collars— with a dry hat under my helmet, I managed to stay, if not warm, comfortable for the remainder of the day. On the other hand, had I dallied in the water in that outfit for very long, it would have lost its protective capacity (see Chapter Four, The Basics of River Rescue).

Responding to Hypothermia

The onset of hypothermia can be either abrupt or gradual. If you dump your boat, fall in, or otherwise get immersed, you're likely to get cold fast. On the other hand, over the course of a cool or rainy day, when conditions may be ripe for hypothermia, the progression to hypothermia may be more subtle. In either case, you should act decisively to prevent, or where necessary, reverse hypothermia.

Immersion. If one of your party ends up in the water on a cold-water or cold-weather day, pull into shore and get the dunkee dry and, if necessary, rewarmed. Don't wait until the symptoms of serious hypothermia (lack of coordination, sluggishness, etc.) set in. Had the party on the North Fork of the Flathead taken that precaution, they might have avoided catastrophe.

Cool Weather. Monitor each other as the day progresses. If someone starts to exhibit even the early phases (e.g., shivering), pull into shore and get warm. Layer your clothes up and down according to the weather, and remember to eat and drink steadily throughout the day— keep fueled and hydrated.

Treatment of Hypothermia

If the victim is conscious and rational, give him warm drinks, food, dry clothes, and shelter from the wind. If necessary, build a fire to help the victim warm up.

If the victim is unable to help himself, undress the victim and place him in a sleeping bag or blanket with another person, skin-to-skin (as in "naked") to rewarm the victim's core temperature. In this case, it is important to rewarm the body's main core before the extremities.

Important—When the victim experiences severe hypothermia, handle him as gently as possible. Rough treatment could trigger ventricular fibrillation and kill him.

Cardinal Rules for Preventing Hypothermia

1. Dress to anticipate hypothermia. Bring enough layers to anticipate changes in weather and temperature, and remove or add layers as needed. Avoid cotton clothing, which wicks warmth from your body when it gets wet.

2. Eat and drink to prevent hypothermia. Eat and drink small amounts frequently, even if you don't feel like doing it.

3. Monitor yourself and others in your group for signs of hypothermia, and treat any signs or symptoms as soon as you see them. When necessary, get off the river.

The Third Deadly Mistake
Operator Inexperience

The accident report forms that the Montana Department of Fish, Wildlife, and Parks uses have a section called "Operator Experience." This section gauges the experience of the person or persons operating both the type of boat involved in the accident and any other craft. This section measures experience in hourly increments—under twenty hours, twenty to one hundred hours, one hundred to five hundred hours, and over five hundred hours. While one might quibble with whether this is an appropriate breakdown of experience, the reports in which this section is filled out (not every report included this information) are instructive. Of the thirty-eight reports reviewed, seventeen of the accidents involved people with less than one hundred hours experience.

Perhaps as telling, of all the accidents, regardless of hours of operator experience, only seven boaters claimed any formal training in boating. Twenty years of experience doing something the wrong way doesn't count for much in a crisis.

Inexperience manifests itself in these accident reports in a number of ways, ranging from inadequate preparation for cold water and weather (note the North Fork of the Flathead accident) to failure to wear a PFD, to inability to judge the difficulty of the water conditions, to inability to maneuver the craft. A few examples illustrate the consequences of inexperience.

A Drowning at Roundup Rapids on the Blackfoot

On May 17, 1992, Chris and Craig launched their canoe on the Blackfoot River at the confluence of the Blackfoot and the Clearwater. A few miles downstream, they capsized in Roundup Rapid, just upstream from the Highway 200 bridge. When the boat tipped, Craig was thrown clear and made it to shore. Chris hung on to the canoe, which then wrapped around a rock. While it isn't precisely clear what happened next, Chris appeared to be trapped between the canoe and the rock. An initial attempt to rescue Chris by another boat failed because of the rough water.

When Chris was finally pulled from the water, the rescuers discovered that his shoe lace had caught on an eyebolt that he had installed on the deck of the canoe.

A number of things stand out about this incident. First, the two paddlers were novices. By the survivor's account, they had been down the Bitterroot and Clark Fork Rivers a total of four times.

Second, Roundup Rapid is a class II to III rapid characterized by large and irregular waves. It is not novice water. The difficulty of the rapid is compounded by the high water of mid-May. Finally, on this particular day, the water temperature was approximately 50 degrees F. The paddlers did not scout the rapid.

Third, the paddlers were ill-equipped to run whitewater. The boat had no flotation bags in it. Neither paddler was wearing a life jacket.

Fourth, the paddlers were boating alone.

Finally, Chris apparently had no training in how to react to an upset in a rapid, as suggested by the fact that he may have been pinned for a time between the boat and the rock.

Primary Factors Contributing to the Accident:

1. Inexperience. A number of factors led to this accident, all of them the result of the paddlers' inexperience.

First, the paddlers were apparently self-taught, with only a few trips to their credit. Their inability to navigate the boat in the rapid was the most immediate cause of their accident.

2. Failure to scout. Second, they should have scouted the rapid. The exercise of scouting might have persuaded them to portage or line around the rapid. On the other hand, given their relative inexperience, they might not have known how to scout even if they'd tried.

Primary Factors Contributing to the Fatality:

1. Inexperience and lack of formal instruction. Although the cause of the fatality, on its face, seems obvious—drowning—Chris's inexperience and lack of formal instruction were likely major factors in his becoming trapped and drowning. Even a basic course (or, for that matter, a guided whitewater paddle-raft trip) would have taught him the proper defensive response to avoid getting trapped in rough water—namely, don't remain downstream of your boat once you're in the water.

2. Failure to wear a PFD. A secondary cause of the fatality was the lack of a PFD. Had Chris worn a properly fitted PFD, he likely would have floated higher in the water and been better able to maneuver. Again, inexperience nudged him toward a fatal mistake.

The Cardinal Rules for Overcoming Inexperience

1. Get expert instruction in the use of your craft, whether from a knowledgeable friend or acquaintance, or from a trained instructor.

2. Once you've received some training in the use of your chosen craft, *practice*. See Chapter Three, Navigation.

3. Learn how to read rivers, how to identify hazards, and how to avoid hazards. (This book is a good place to start.)

4. Don't be ashamed to admit your limitations. Don't allow others in a group to pressure you into trying something you don't want to do. It may literally mean your life.

The Fourth Deadly Mistake
Use of Alcohol and Drugs on the River

Beer floats—armadas of rafts, often trailing inner tubes or smaller rafts full of beer, and drifting aimlessly down the river—are a cliché on western rivers. You know immediately when you have come upon a beer float. The mood will be raucous, though usually friendly. Lots of splashing and falling overboard commonly attend these events. And all too often, there's not a PFD in sight.

Less intrusive but perhaps more widespread is the time-honored custom of loading up the cooler with beer and sipping (or quaffing) steadily while fishing or running the rapids.

In either case, these behaviors are a formula for disaster. In many of the fatal accidents that have occurred, alcohol was a factor, if not the leading factor. It can sometimes be difficult to weigh the contribution of alcohol to a boating accident. In many cases, it is one of a number of factors. But the effects of alcohol can be so insidious and pervasive—especially in impairing one's judgment and reflexes—that it is no surprise that the presence of alcohol at boating accidents appears repeatedly. Sometimes the results are disastrous even on flat water, as illustrated by the incidents described below.

A Double Drowning on Flathead Lake

In early April 1996, two men took a canoe out on Flathead Lake. It was a clear, mild (50 degrees F) day with a light wind and light chop. The water was extremely cold (35 degrees F). The two canoeists never returned. Searchers recovered their bodies much later; they died from drowning. Nobody knows what happened to cause the accident, but we do know this about the paddlers:

1. They had less than twenty hours experience in the canoe;

2. they apparently had been drinking heavily (they had blood alcohol levels of .15 and .17 respectively); and

3. neither was wearing a PFD at the time of the accident.

Primary Factor Contributing to the Accident:

Drinking and inexperience. Given the combination of heavy drinking and inexperience, it's reasonable to attribute the accident to those two factors alone. It is a deadly combination.

Primary Factors Contributing to the Fatalities:

1. Failure to wear a PFD. Here, the lack of PFD was certainly a factor.

2. Hypothermia. As cold as the water was, and given that nobody was nearby to assist them, they likely would have succumbed to hypothermia even if they had worn PFDs.

3. Boating alone. A third factor is that they were alone. Had they gone out with another boat, the other boat might have been able to assist them when they capsized.

Another Double Drowning on Flathead Lake

In late April 1993, after partying all night with friends, two men still under the influence headed out on Flathead Lake for an early-morning paddle. Later tests showed that they had blood alcohol levels of .28 and .11 respectively—most people with a blood alcohol level of .28 would be falling-down drunk. Shortly after embarking, they capsized. Approximately a half hour after starting out, they both washed up on the beach, dead. They were both wearing PFDs, and their heads were out of the water. Authorities concluded that they died of hypothermia, and not drowning.

The air temperature on that day was approximately 50 degrees F and the water was 49 degrees F. The water was calm, and the wind was light.

Besides being under the influence of alcohol, the two paddlers had virtually no experience in a canoe (less than twenty hours) and no formal instruction between them.

Primary Factor Contributing to the Accident:

Alcohol and inexperience: Given the absolutely calm conditions on the water, the only possible conclusion is that, again, the deadly combination of inexperience and alcohol combined to cause this accident. A canoe can be unforgiving to a first-time boater in the best of times. Add large amounts of alcohol and impair the boater's coordination and judgment, and you have a lethal mix.

Primary Factors Contributing to the Fatalities:

1. Hypothermia. Early season paddling or floating often is a high-probability time for hypothermia. Had the victims dressed properly for the water temperatures (a wet suit or dry suit or layers of the correct clothing), they might have increased their chances of survival. On the other hand, it may have simply delayed the inevitable.

2. Boating alone. Had there been another boat on the outing, however, a rescue before the onset of hypothermia might have saved these paddlers. Paddling alone comes with the added risk that, if you get into trouble, there's no one else to help you. Sadly, in both of these instances, that was the case.

The Cardinal Rule of Drugs and Alcohol on the Water

Don't

While you're on the water, do not use alcohol or drugs.

The Fifth Deadly Mistake
The Victims Were Non-swimmers

Thus far, most of the fatal accidents have involved people with at least some swimming skills. A victim's plight only worsens if he or she cannot swim.

Drowning on the Swan

On July 4, 1989, Susan, Larry, and Susan's two children (six and ten years old) attempted to float the Swan River about a mile east of Big Fork in a twelve-foot canoe. This reach of the Swan River is tough, technical whitewater too difficult for all but the most expert canoeists. It has killed more than one experienced paddler. The boat swamped about five hundred yards from the put-in. The man and two children managed to get to shore. Susan did not, and searchers found her body the next day.

This particular reach of the Swan is widely known to be extremely dangerous. It is a difficult swim even for accomplished swimmers. Susan was known to be a poor swimmer (there is some conflict in the report—in one place she is characterized as a non-swimmer; in another as a "poor swimmer"). Of the four occupants, only Susan had on a PFD. Larry and Susan collectively had almost no experience in a canoe (the report listed their experience as "under twenty hours"). Under "formal training," the report inexplicably listed "self taught."

The day was clear and warm (85 degrees F), but the water was estimated to be approximately 50 degrees F.

Primary Factors Contributing to the Accident:

1. Inexperience. This group was an accident waiting to happen. They lacked the boating skills for even a gentle section of the river.

2. Lack of judgment. The outing was doomed the moment these people made the decision to run this section of the Swan. Clearly they lacked the experience to understand how dangerous and demanding this reach of water is. Under the circumstances, it's a minor miracle that they did not all drown.

3. Inadequate equipment and equipment improperly used. Further evidence of this group's inexperience shows up in (a) their choice of craft, and (b) their loading of the craft beyond capacity. A twelve-foot canoe of any design will not handle well in any water with four people in it, much less in difficult whitewater like this stretch of the Swan. Further, water this technical demands specialized craft and equipment to handle it. From the information included in the report, this canoe was not designed for this kind of water.

Primary Factors Contributing to the Fatality:

1. Cold Water. The water temperature was 50 degrees F. Any extended time in water that cold is certainly going to result in hypothermia. The loss of strength and coordination that accompany hypothermia certainly would have contributed to her predicament, even if she had known how to swim.

2. Non-swimmer. In heavy rapids, your only hope for survival may be your own ability to self-rescue by defensive swimming. Rapids can be difficult to swim in any circumstance, especially if you haven't had any training in how to swim them safely. Given the total lack of experience of this group, and the woman's history as a poor or non-swimmer, her chances of performing any kind of self-rescue were negligible, and ultimately, her chances of survival were slim, even with a PFD. It's notable that the other people in the boat—who could swim—survived.

Advice for Non-swimmers

As the Swan River instance makes clear, being able to swim may be crucial to your survival even if you wear a PFD. One of the cardinal principles of getting yourself out of trouble is the ability to function in the water when you are out of your boat. If you don't have at least basic swimming skills, you aren't likely to be able to help yourself once you're out of the boat.

Swimming skills are important on another level. If you can swim, your time on the water will be more enjoyable, because the ability to swim can remove the apprehension of anticipating an upset. River running doesn't have to have all the dread-induced tension of a death sport, and learning to swim will go a long way towards reducing that tension.

Cardinal Rules for Non-swimmers
1. Learn to swim.
2. If you can't swim, wear a properly fitting PFD. (Even if you can swim, don't forget to wear your PFD.)
3. Learn to swim.
4. If you can't swim, stay on calm, flat water close to shore.
5. Learn to swim.

The five deadly mistakes are, simply, avoidable hazards. Banish these mistakes from your river repertoire, and you are well on your way to being a safe boater.

Chapter Two
Reading the Water

I n Chapter One, we looked at the subjective factors that get people into trouble on the water. In virtually every case, those subjective dangers boil down to one thing—a failure of judgment. But how can you exercise judgment without experience and without knowing what to avoid in the way of objective hazards on a river? You can't.

River reading is a learned skill. This chapter will introduce the objective features that you run into on any river—currents, gradients, eddies, downstream Vs, waves, holes, ledges, dams, sweepers, and strainers. We'll talk about the major hazards, how to avoid those hazards (basic rules of navigation), and how to escape those hazards once you're in them.

This chapter will give you some idea of what to look for. But only by spending time on the river, learning to read the signs that identify the hazards and the routes, will you be able to acquire river-reading skills.

Basic River Hydrology

Certain characteristics will be the same from one river to the next the world over. Simply understanding these characteristics can go a long way toward keeping you out of trouble on the water.

Current. The most obvious feature of any river is its current—moving water. Current speed is one of the most compelling features of any river; the faster a river's current, the thinner your margin of error.

Current speed is primarily the product of three things:

1. volume of water moving past a given point,

2. river width, and

3. river gradient.

There are other influences on current speed, but these three factors have the greatest effect on any river's current.

Volume is most often expressed as cubic feet per second (cfs). Cfs expresses the amount of water flowing past a fixed point in one second. One cfs equals 448 gallons per minute (consider that your average household faucet yields anywhere from five to ten gallons per minute, and you'll realize that one cfs is a fair amount of water).

River volume can be a deceptive standard. You need to take into account both river width and gradient to really understand the influence of volume on current speed. What would be a high volume of water on one river can be a trickle on another. For example, when the Missouri River in the section designated as "wild and scenic" flows at 10,000 cfs, it is still relatively slow moving. On the other hand, when the Smith River in Montana is flowing at 2,000 cfs, it is flying. The difference? The Missouri is a wide, flat (low gradient) prairie river, while the Smith is a steep and narrow river.

River width. A river's width can drastically alter the relative speed and turbulence of a current—generally, the narrower the width, the faster the current. By way of illustration, consider what happens when you clamp your thumb over the end of a common garden hose. The relatively gentle flow suddenly accelerates and the range of the spray increases dramatically. By constricting the flow, you have narrowed the "width between the banks" of the hose, increasing current velocity. The next time you are on a river whose banks suddenly close in, note the effect this narrowing has on current speed.

River gradient. Gradient is the steepness of the riverbed, expressed in "feet per mile" (fpm). A river that has an average gradient of 30 fpm will likely be a wild, fast ride. A river that drops an average of 10 fpm will be much gentler, for the most part. One cautionary note, however. River gradient is usually described as an *average* for a given river. A river with an average gradient of 10 fpm may have some short stretches where the gradient is 50 fpm. Those stretches will likely have some serious rapids. The portion of the Colorado that passes through the Grand Canyon is a good example. The moral? Look beyond the averages. Look to good river guidebooks or topographical maps that will show you those abrupt changes in gradient.

All three of these features can influence current speed. Put all three of them together in the right (or wrong) combination—high volume, narrow banks, and steep gradient—and you have a raging torrent. It's better to go for a hike, read a good book, floss your teeth, or do anything *else* on those days.

There are other influences on current speed that are universal to any river. Knowing them can help you keep out of a current you'd rather avoid.

Current on river bends. Perhaps the most important of these influences is the tendency of the current to move faster on the outside of a river bend than on the inside of the bend.

On a sharp bend, the water on the outside seems to go right into the bank at the bend of the river. A common way to avoid getting your boat

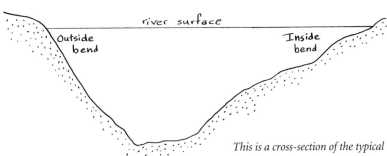

This is a cross-section of the typical bend in the river. On the left, the outside of the bend, the water is typically deeper and the current moves faster. On the inside of the bend (on right), the river tends to be shallower and the current moves slower.

smashed into the bank in such a situation is to sneak to the inside of the bend, where the water is slower.

Friction. A less obvious influence on current speed is friction. We tend to think of friction in the dry-land context, e.g., rubbing your hands together to create heat—but friction can also influence water flow. On the straight sections of a river, regardless of the volume of its flow, a river's current moves slower close to the banks and along the bottom (although a river's bottom is not likely where you want to experience the benefits of friction). Banks and bottom provide the friction that slows the current.

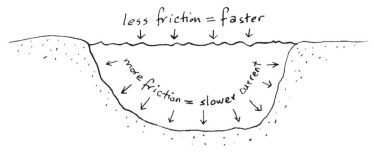

Friction causes the current to move slower along the banks and the bottom. If you're looking for slower water, look to the river's edge. But don't forget that, on river bends, the outside of the turn will be faster than the inside.

Identifying Specific River Features

There are a number of features in all rivers that can help you find the safest route down a river. Learn how to identify these features. While this guide can help you know what to look for, the only place you can learn these things is on the water.

Downstream Vs. As you look downstream at any place where a river narrows, or where there are obstacles in the river, tongues of relatively glassy water form inverted Vs (with the base of the V pointing downstream). These downstream Vs—in some circles, you'll hear the downstream V called the "tongue"— indicate the deepest, clearest paths of water. Where a river is relatively shallow, the largest downstream V will offer your best chance for going through the shallow without getting stranded on the bottom.

In some cases, the downstream V is obvious. Most of the time, however, the downstream V won't be so easy to see, especially from boat level. When the water is shallow, the "V" may look more like a "U." In really windy conditions, the V can be just plain hard to see. Spotting the V takes practice. Two common variations of the downstream V appear in the following four photographs. The next time you are on a river or stream, look for the Vs and look for the variations in their appearance.

Can you see the V in this picture? In places where the river is uniformly shallow, the V might not be so obvious.

In fact, as shown by the markings on this photo, the "V" may look more like a "U" or may be nothing more that a slight variation in the profile of the current. Learn to look for those variations.

In busy water with lots of rocks and obstacles, you won't have the luxury of one nice long V. Instead you look for lots of smaller, subtle Vs. Can you find a route through this mess? After you read about holes and horizon lines, come back and look at the picture again and see if you can find the holes and ledges.

As you can see from the markings on this photo, there are a multitude of Vs here, but not necessarily in a straight line.

Eddies. Eddies are found behind rocks, trees, or other obstacles in streams. Because an obstacle blocks the downstream current from entering the space directly below it, water flows in from below the space, creating an upstream current. This upstream current is the eddy.

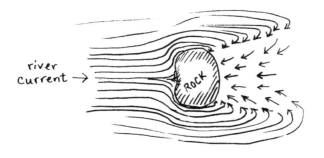

While it doesn't always seem like it, the water below the rock is actually flowing back upstream as it fills the vacuum created by the rock.

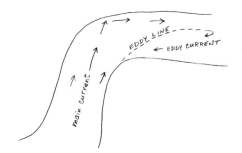

Below every inside bend on a river, there will be an eddy. On a narrow, fast-moving river that eddy can be your best friend.

Any rock that pokes above the water surface will form an eddy. Likewise, any obstruction that projects out from the bank will form an eddy. The inside of a bend on a river will always form an eddy downstream of the bend.

Why are eddies important? For a number of reasons. An eddy can be both a blessing and a curse to river runners. First, an eddy can provide a resting place, or safe haven, in the middle of moving water. Second, the upstream current can create a hazard for unwitting boaters when they cross into or out of an eddy. Third, if you unwittingly enter an eddy, it can impede your progress down a river.

Experienced canoeists and kayakers are well acquainted with the benefits of eddies. Canoeists and kayakers both learn to cross out of the downstream current and into the eddy, performing an "eddy turn." Experienced boaters of all stripes—whether in a canoe, kayak, raft, or drift boat—also know how to back ferry, or set, into eddies. See Chapter Three, Navigation, for a discussion of eddy turns and setting.

Waves versus holes. Any given feature in a river may present itself differently at different flows. For example, a big rock that rises above the surface at low water may create a wave at high water levels, or a hole at medium water levels. At extremely high water, you may see no evidence of it at all. Understanding what causes waves and holes and how to identify them from upstream can save you a lot of grief. As a practical matter, it is not always possible to tell, from upstream, whether an obstruction is causing a wave or a hole. If you're not sure, go around it.

The horizon line for a hole and a wave may look a lot alike. If you're not sure what you're approaching—hole or wave— pull over and scout.

Waves. We tend to think of waves as features of rapids, and yet they can occur almost anywhere on a river. Generally, waves occur where faster moving water piles up on slower moving water.

In the example of the rock above, at certain water levels, the rock creates a steeper (if momentary) gradient over which the water speeds up. When that water piles into the slower water below the rock, a wave forms. From upstream, the water surface will appear as a short, relatively straight horizon with turbulence below it.

Waves will also occur where there is a compression that increases the velocity of the water. If you have enough water volume and current

If a wave's crest breaks back upstream on itself, you're looking at a "stopper."

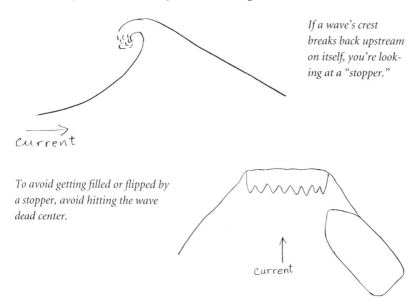

To avoid getting filled or flipped by a stopper, avoid hitting the wave dead center.

current

velocity, you may see a series of waves formed. Often, in these cases, the downstream V goes right into the wave train.

Some waves will be so steep that the crest of the wave will break and fall back upstream. These waves are known as "stoppers." When these waves are large, they can fill or flip a boat. One way to avoid that consequence is to try to hit a shoulder of the wave instead of striking it dead center.

Holes. Holes occur when water drops vertically over or around an obstruction such as a rock. The obstruction creates a void in the river that the current fills by flowing back on itself, somewhat like an eddy. This backflow creates an upstream current below the obstruction that eventually flows out the bottom or side of the void. Unlike an eddy, the

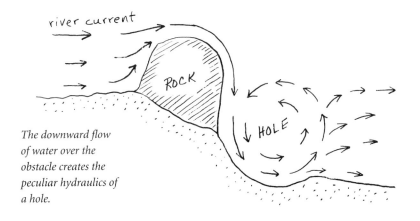

The downward flow of water over the obstacle creates the peculiar hydraulics of a hole.

downward flow of water over the obstacle and into the hole can hold things in the hole. Holes can range from minor interruptions of the current to boat-eating hydraulics that can fill your boat or even flip it.

Because of the destructive potential of big holes, it is important to be able to recognize them from upstream. As with certain waves, holes will often appear as a flat, abnormal horizon line on the river's surface, with no immediate view of the water directly below the horizon line.

On large holes, the river's surface may actually bulge above the surrounding water. We call this bulge the "pillow." If the pillow is large enough, it is sometimes sufficient to deflect your craft away from the hole. You may not want to depend on the deflective force of the pillow, however.

The pillow on a big rock or over a hole may be big enough to keep you off the rock. From upstream, the water will actually seem to rise up slightly above the level of the water around you. That's your pillow. If the water going into a rock or bank seems to slope down into the rock or the back, stay away, it may be undercut.

River-Reading Training Aid
You don't have to surrender yourself to the maw of the wildest river around to study the kinds of features discussed in this chapter. You can do it safely, and in miniature. Go to a small creek near where you live, preferably one with a rocky bottom. There you can see, in miniature—and at no significant threat to yourself—virtually any river feature you can think of, from eddies to downstream Vs, to holes, to falls. If you don't see exactly the feature you want, build it yourself, using a hand, a foot, a leg, or maybe a few small rocks (but don't conduct a major excavation of the stream bed), or a piece of wood.

River Hazards

There are a number of features that you are likely to encounter that can be fairly classified as objective hazards. These include strainers, waves, undercut rocks or banks, eddies, holes, ledges, and low-head dams. We have discussed the identification of some of these above. This section will discuss those hazards and additional ones and will recommend ways to escape if you find yourself caught in them.

Strainers. Strainers are trees or other obstacles that fall or get washed into the river, leaving part of the obstacle above the surface and part below the surface. The current washes through and under a strainer.

The classic strainer is a tree fallen into the river from the bank. The other common form of strainer, especially in wooded areas of the country, is a logjam.

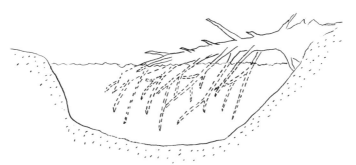

Fallen trees are the most common kind of strainer. You can see them on almost any stream or river. They are especially ubiquitous in the spring, when high water undercuts banks and drops trees into the river. Because they are so common, they may pose the greatest danger to the recreational floater.

Death in a Logjam on the Clark Fork

On June, 1992, five people, Phil, Jenny, Bob, Dave, and Linda, capsized their raft at a logjam on the Clark Fork River west of Missoula. Jenny became trapped in the logjam and drowned. Jenny, although a non-swimmer, was wearing a PFD.

The river at the site of the accident was running at a moderate current, and the weather was clear.

Several in the party had been drinking, and they apparently made no effort to avoid the jam.

Primary Factors Contributing to the Accident:

1. Alcohol use and operator inexperience. It is immediately apparent that this group broke many of the basic rules described in Chapter One, with alcohol being a prime factor in the accident. At least three of the five rafters had been drinking. Alcohol not only impairs one's judgment, but also one's reflexes. Here, the heavy use of alcohol suggests that this party simply did not have enough river experience to understand the consequences associated with heavy drinking on a river.

2. Operator inattention. In this instance, the obstacle was—by all accounts— relatively easy to avoid. Nonetheless, the people in the raft did little to avoid it. To an inexperienced boater, a logjam may seem like an innocuous obstacle. Someone with sufficient experience or training, however, would recognize the hazard posed by such a strainer and make every effort to avoid it. Again, had their judgment not been impaired by alcohol, these rafters might have been more alert to the hazards on the river.

Primary Factor Contributing to the Fatality:

Entanglement in a strainer. The primary cause of death in this case was drowning—but drowning caused by entanglement in an avoidable strainer. It was apparent that Jenny, a non-swimmer, made no effort to avoid the entrapment. (1) Had she been a swimmer, she would have had a better chance to escape the jam, and (2) had she been trained in proper escape from strainers caused by such things as logjams, she might have survived.

A Close Call on the Snake

In the summer of 1973, while working as a seasonal park employee on an entrance gate in Grand Teton National Park, I got an assigned-duty day (an institutional excuse to do something besides your job) with the river ranger. We launched at the mouth of Pacific Creek mid-morning on a warm, clear day. Ed, the ranger, took his job—and my neophyte presence in his boat—seriously. Quickly and concisely, he ran me through the rules of behavior on the river.

A mile or so from the start, we came around a bend. Several hundred yards down on the next bend, we could see a huge logjam. Floating toward it (and, as it turned out, into it) was a yellow rubber ducky just like the one from my culvert experience. Ed tried to yell a warning to them, but they were too far below us to hear it.

Anticipating the wreck, Ed put the raft into high gear, spinning us around and pulling downstream. I watched as the raft first piled into the jam and then suddenly disappeared. I could see one person on top of the jam and the head and shoulders of another just on the upstream side. A minute or so after they hit (it seemed an eternity), Ed pulled us to the upstream side of the jam, and, on his instruction, we both hopped immediately onto the jam and pulled our raft onto the top of the jam.

The man on top of the jam was trying to hold his friend's head out of the water, but it was clear that he was losing the battle. The current was sucking most of the man's body under the jam. Moving quickly, Ed placed me on the swimmer's left shoulder and he got on his right shoulder. At his count, we grabbed the man's horse-collar PFD and anything else we could grip—and we tugged. The swimmer budged up a few inches, but his PFD chafed against the logs and made it tough going. After several more tries, gaining a few inches each time, we finally managed to pull him out onto the jam. In the water for no more than five minutes, he was completely spent and unable to help himself even to sit up. We found items of their gear for several miles downstream. Their raft never did come out of the logjam.

Primary Factors Contributing to the Accident:

The cause of this accident was two-fold—first, the obvious hazard of the logjam, and second, the rafters' total lack of boating experience. Hearing how scenic the Snake was, they had borrowed the raft and headed down river. They simply did not realize the power of the current into the log-jam and therefore made no effort to avoid it. Under the circumstances, they got off lightly.

To the inexperienced boater, many strainers—whether they are a fallen tree or a logjam—won't look especially threatening. Often the water just seems to flow up to them and around them. Don't be deceived. The most dangerous part of the strainer is the part you can't see. In most cases (and, to be safe, assume *all* cases), strainers have appendages that extend below the surface. These appendages can catch and, as the Clark Fork and Snake River incidents above illustrate, hold anything that the current brings to them, including you or your boat. The force of the pressure that water exerts per square inch is enormous, and once tangled in a strainer, you will find it virtually impossible to extricate yourself. Your best tactic is to avoid all strainers.

Self-rescue from a strainer. So what should you do when, having ignored my sage advice, you fail to avoid a strainer? Whether you are swimming or still in the boat, your response should be the same. Climb as high onto the strainer as you can.

The prevailing pull of the current through the strainer is down. The current will suck a boat or a person that simply drifts into a strainer under the surface and into the strainer. Once your legs get downstream ahead of you at the top of a strainer, it is unbelievably difficult to pull yourself out of the strainer. Likewise, once part of your boat goes under, your chances of getting it out intact are slim to none. So, again, before you get sucked under, you need to do everything you can to get yourself and your boat out of the water and onto the strainer well above the water's surface.

Swimming to a strainer. Elsewhere in this book, I will discuss defensive swimming in a rapid; in that case, you should keep on your back and keep your feet facing downstream to fend off obstacles. You have to do just the opposite to avoid getting pulled under a strainer.

1. When you realize that you can't swim clear of a strainer, turn and swim as aggressively as you can *toward* the strainer.

If you're out of your boat and in the water and can't avoid a strainer, swim into it. Don't start so soon that you wear out and lose your momentum before you get there. But then again, don't wait too long, or you may not build enough momentum.

2. When you arrive at the strainer, place your hands out in front of you and pull yourself up onto the strainer. Kick vigorously to help propel yourself up onto the strainer and to help keep your feet from getting pulled under.

When you get to the strainer, pull yourself up and kick like mad. Don't stop kicking until your legs are mostly out of the water. Even a slight hesitation can kill your momentum and pull you back in.

It is much easier to describe this maneuver than it is to perform it. You can practice by suspending a piece of PVC pipe in the river at the surface and then swimming down to it (in a life jacket) and pulling yourself over it. Of course, if you can't swim, you probably won't have a chance of completing this maneuver, and you'll get sucked into the strainer and likely drown.

Exiting your boat onto a strainer. When you realize that you aren't going to be able to avoid a strainer with your boat, prepare to disembark the moment your boat touches the strainer. If you are in a raft or a drift boat, turn your boat perpendicular to the current and get everyone to the downstream side.

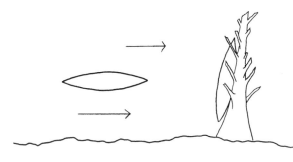

When you can't avoid the strainer, align your boat perpendicular to the current and be ready to climb out on the strainer as soon as the boat gets there.

If you are in a canoe or a kayak, turn your boat perpendicular to the current and tilt your boat to the downstream side when you arrive at the strainer. *Do not lean your craft upstream. Leaning upstream will seal your doom.*

When the boat touches the strainer, vault onto the strainer. If you can pull your boat up with you, so much the better (although you'll have to vault and pull at the same time). But remember, the boat is replaceable. You are not. If trying to rescue the boat puts you at risk, let the boat go.

Make sure you have that downstream lean.

Cardinal Rules on Strainers

1. Avoid strainers at all costs.

2. If you are out of your boat and cannot avoid going into the strainer, swim aggressively toward the strainer, and when you get to it, pull yourself up onto the tree, logjam, or other object forming the strainer.

3. If you are in your boat and you cannot avoid the strainer, align the boat to the strainer so that you and your passengers may exit the boat onto the strainer. Tilt the boat toward the strainer.

4. Pull your boat up onto the strainer *only if you can do so without personal risk to yourself.*

Kayak on a Strainer

A kayak, with its sealed cockpit, offers a special challenge to exiting onto a strainer. As with all other craft, the best strategy is to stay away (This applies in spades to any decked, skirted boat). But, if you cannot simply avoid the strainer, you have two options, neither of which is great.

The first option depends on how high the strainer rises out of the water. If the strainer is a low-lying tree trunk or some other obstacle which slopes gradually out of the river, you can try paddling your boat up onto the strainer by leaning back in your boat (to get the bow as high as possible) and paddling as fast as you can toward it, maintaining your speed as you climb up on it. This is the same idea as the swimmer swimming up on it.

If the strainer is too high out of the water or emerges too steeply out of the water, option one won't work. In that case, option two is a variation of the tactic used by other boats in a similar predicament. If you can't paddle onto the strainer, turn your boat sideways to it, and as you get to it, lean downstream (showing the current the bottom of your boat), and pull yourself up onto the strainer. If you can do it without popping out of the cockpit, good for you. But remember, it's a lot easier to replace the boat than it is to replace you.

Sweepers. A sweeper is a bankside feature—most commonly a tree or trees—that has fallen over the river. Branches or other appendages hang down toward the water. If you happen to go through a sweeper, it may remove you from your craft. (When the limbs of a sweeper go all the way into the water, you have a strainer.) Sweepers often occur on the outside of bends, because the water flowing into the outside of the bend tends to undercut trees and dump them into the river. So, a good tactic for avoiding sweepers is to hold your craft to the inside of a bend. This keeps you out of the prevailing current and therefore out of the sweeper. See Chapter Three, Navigation.

Low-head Dams

A Drowning at a Low-head Dam on the Milk River

In northern Montana, the Milk River winds across flat hay and wheat land to join with the Missouri near Glasgow. It would seem to be the perfect river for a lazy spring float. In late May 1991, four men set out for what they thought would be just such a trip.

If was a warm (73 degrees F), though gusty day, and the water, while high, was relatively warm for May (54 degrees F). The four men set out just above Havre and, unbeknownst to them, above the Havre city water weir. The weir is simply a low-head dam that diverts water from the Milk River. The rafters were unaware of its existence.

The accident report indicates that when the rafters saw the weir, they put on their life jackets. There is no indication that they made any attempt to get to shore and portage around the weir. One rafter jumped out of the raft before it went over the weir, and he was swept into the hydraulic below the weir. The raft followed and became trapped with the other three men aboard.

The man overboard circulated several times through the hydraulic until his PFD came off. Eventually the hydraulic flushed him downstream. His companions were able to jump over the pillow of water at the lower end of the hydraulic and swim after their companion. They retrieved him, but were unable to revive him. He was later pronounced dead at Northern Hospital in Havre.

Primary Factors Contributing to the Accident:

Operator inexperience and inattention. The primary cause of this accident is pretty straightforward. First, the floaters weren't aware of the hazard, and when they became aware of it, they either took no action to avoid it or were unable to avoid it. Clearly, had they been aware of the hazard, they could have started their float below it or, at least, anticipated the need to portage it.

Avoid low-head dams at all costs. As illustrated here, they come by their nickname, "drowning machine," honestly. The most insidious thing about many low-head dams is that they look innocuous. Worse, the steep, smooth ramp into the hydraulic offers the appeal of a water slide; and the hydraulic doesn't usually look all that bad. It is.

A low-head dam creates a hole with no escape valve. As with a hole, water pours over a low-head dam in a nearly vertical trajectory, creating a recycling current. Unlike most naturally formed holes, however, low-head dams usually have some kind of apron (often concrete) at the sides that blocks off any escape to the side. As a result, once you're trapped in the hydraulic of a low-head dam, it is difficult, if not impossible, to get out.

This is the classic hole below the low-head dam.

The surviving Milk River rafters were unbelievably lucky. They could just as easily have circulated in the weir's hydraulic until it pulled their boat apart and drowned them.

Can you see the horizon line in this photo? This is the approach to the low head dam shown above. When you see that horizon line, get out and go around it.

Avoid low-head dams like the plague. To avoid them, you have to recognize them. Like a hole, the lip of a low-head dam creates a straight horizon line. The difference from a hole is that the horizon line of a low-head dam extends most or all the way across the river. When you see that horizon line, get out of the river well above the horizon line and scout the dam. If there is no downstream V which would allow you to pass safely over the dam, then portage it.

Attempted rescue from a low-head dam. In the history of boat accidents at low-head dams, many people have drowned attempting to rescue other people caught in them. The hydraulic below a low-head dam is so powerful that a rescue boat that approaches a low-head dam from downstream and gets too close will be pulled into the hydraulic.

Four Rescuers Die at a Low-head Dam in Ohio*

A canoeist got caught in a low-head dam on a river in Ohio. The local fire department responded in boats. One rowboat with three rescuers approached the victim from below the hydraulic. When the victim grabbed onto the pole that one of the rescuers extended to him, the hydraulic pulled the rescue boat into the face of the dam and it capsized, trapping the rescuers in the hydraulic. A second boat tried to rescue the first boat and likewise got pulled into the hydraulic. In addition to the canoeist, three rescuers drowned in the hydraulic.

*This incident is graphically depicted in the video, *The Drowning Machine*. See the bibliography.

Primary Factor(s) Contributing to the Accident:

1. Poor understanding of the hydraulics created by low-head dams. Notwithstanding the evident power of the hydraulic holding the victim in the dam, the rescuers did not recognize the boil line marking the hydraulic and therefore didn't understand just how far downstram the hydraulic reached.

2. Poor preparation. The mistake the rescuers made was that they entered the hydraulic with no downstream tether. Without such a tether, they couldn't be pulled away from the hydraulic.

Cardinal Rules on Low-head Dams

As a result of the this incident and a spate of others like it, the State of Ohio developed a number of procedures for rescuing boaters from low-head dams, both from the shore and from boats. This program has become a model in river rescue training. The key to the Ohio procedures is practice. The average recreational boater is not likely to have access to the proper training in these procedures, the necessary equipment, or the ability to practice them. But Ohio's experience suggests some important rules for even the casual recreational floater to follow:

1. Never go into the hydraulic of a low-head dam to rescue someone else.

2. To the extent that you can attempt a rescue, do it from shore, making sure you do not place yourself at risk of being pulled into the hydraulic.

3. Always send someone to get professional rescue help, *making sure* they describe the scene of the accident as a low-head dam.

Holes. A hole, like a low-head dam, occurs when water pours nearly vertically over an obstacle, creating a reversal in the current that will hold things like boats and people in the hole. Unlike low-head dams, however, most holes will have current going out their sides; this will provide an escape route. These are called "smiling" holes, because, when seen from upstream, the eddy lines point downstream in a "smile." Skilled kayakers and some skilled canoeists will actually seek out holes.

Holes can be extremely dangerous, however, and like a low-head dam hydraulic, recirculate you over and over until you get exhausted and drown. The holes that will do this are called "frowning" holes, mainly because the configuration of the eddy lines (to the extent that they exist) forms a "frown" when seen from upstream.

So how to escape? The first and usually the easiest escape route is out the sides of the hole, where the downstream current passes by. Try to move your boat or swim (if you are out of your boat) to the edge of the hole where you can catch the downstream current and let it pull you out.

Big holes may have a bulge of water that is extremely tough to climb over. In this case, your predicament is much like that of the low-head dam. Your only escape may be to try to dive down to the bottom, catch the bottom current, and swim or flush out the bottom.

Ledges. Ledges can run the gamut from innocuous, waterslide-like ramps to steep drops that create the same kind of hydraulic that you see in a hole or below a low-head dam. In fact, the bad ones are just wide holes. Ledges occur when a riverbed undergoes a sudden elevation drop that extends across all or part of the river. Some of the great whitewater drops and surfing waves in the West involve ledges. The trick is to recognize an approaching ledge before it is too late to scout it.

As with a low-head dam, the diagnostic feature of a ledge is usually a straight horizontal line that marks a sudden drop of the riverbed. If all you can see below the line are the tops of bankside trees or vegetation, get out and scout it—it's probably a steep one.

If you get caught in the hydraulic below the ledge, your escape route is the same as with holes—out the side.

Rocks or other obstacles. Rocks, logs, junk car bodies (these are so common on some rivers that they seem like part of the natural habitat)—or any other obstacles that rise from the bed of the river and break the surface of the water—create hazards that may seem too obvious to mention. While these obstacles may be obvious, they are nonetheless among the most common causes of wrecked boats on rivers throughout the United States.

Certainly, identification is easy. See that house-sized rock up ahead? That's an obstacle. Please try to miss it. If you want to miss it, pay attention. Most people wrap on rocks because they aren't paying any attention. See more about paying attention in Chapter Three, Navigation.

But what if you blew it on the "pay attention" part and now, like it or not, you're going to hit the rock? What do you do? First, don't panic. Depending on the kind of craft you're in, you may be able to extricate yourself from your predicament without looking too stupid.

If you're in a fixed-oar craft or a paddle raft, and if the obstacle isn't too big, you may be able to spin your way around or off the obstacle. And if you time it correctly, you may later be able to convince people that spinning was what you intended to do all along. Here's the drill:

1. If you have any time at all to maneuver, try to get slightly offset from the center of the rock, with the back of the boat nearest the edge of the rock.

2. When you are just a few feet above the rock (far enough above to get your oar or paddles in), pull on the upstream oar (backpaddling in a paddle raft) and push on the downstream oar (forward paddling in a paddle raft), making the boat spin and roll around the rock.

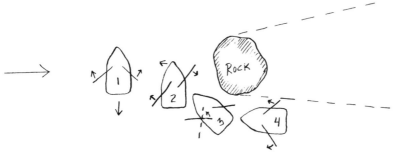

It doesn't take too much offset from the obstacle to set up the boat to spin. You'll want to practice your spinning strokes before you get in this predicament. This is not the time to be learning your right from your left. On a good-sized obstacle, you may get some assist from the pillow above. But if your boat is big and heavy, don't plan on it.

If you are in a canoe, and you can't avoid hitting the rock, try to hit it head-on. That may at least allow you to pendulum off the rock in much the same fashion as you would in the spin technique described above for fixed-oar craft and paddle rafts. As the canoe starts to turn

As the boat starts to swing downstream, resist the temptation to lean upstream. That upstream lean will guarantee a swim.

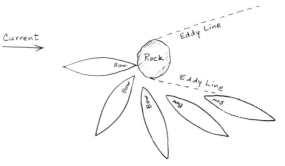

broadside to the current after hitting the rock, do a quick couple of back strokes to clear the front of the canoe off the rock. It won't be very pretty, but it may save you from wrapping your canoe.

But, after all that good advice, you may not be able to do anything except hit the rock sideways. Now your main task is to avoid a complete boat-eating pin. The cardinal rule here is to lean the boat downstream toward the obstacle as you get to it and either try to push off the rock, or if the rock is big enough, get out of your craft, onto the rock, and try to pull your boat up out of the water with you. **Do not lean upstream.** Leaning upstream will assure disaster, allowing the current to tip and fill your boat before it pins it to the rock. This can happen whether you're in a raft, canoe, kayak, or drift boat. If this happens, the best you can hope for is a badly damaged boat (especially if it is a hard-sided craft). In the worst case, you could die and your boat could become a permanent river feature. Talk about embarrassing.

That Demon Upstream Lean

When approaching an obstacle sideways or even simply entering a current that's moving in a different direction, most of us seem to have an innate response—lean upstream. This is the worst possible move. The current that moves our boat downstream does it by hitting and running along the bottom of our boat. In a state of balance, that pressure on the bottom of the boat moves the whole boat downstream at equal speed. When we lose that state of equilibrium—by leaning upstream—the current against the boat bottom effectively moves the bottom faster than the rest of the boat, tipping the upstream gunwale towards the water.

Even hard-sided rowboats, such as drift boats, can tip over if they leave an eddy out of its upstream end. To avoid this in a fixed oar boat,, row out of the downstream end of the eddy, where the contrast between currents is not so great. Or, if you have to enter the main current high on the eddy line, lean downstream as much as you can—sometimes tougher to do in a drift boat.

In a raft, tipping over is less likely to be a problem unless you're piling into a rock or trying to get out of a hole. In a canoe, it nearly always means a swim. See more about leaning on eddy turns in Chapter Three, Navigation.

In the classic "upstream tip" the bottom moves downstream faster than the rest of the boat.

Rating River Difficulty

While numerical systems that rate a river's difficulty don't fall cleanly under the rubric of "reading the water," a river's rating can give some guidance about whether you want to be on the river at all. As a result, you should be aware of these rating systems, have some idea of how they work, and their limitations. There are two systems used in the United States—the International Scale of River Difficulty, established by the American Whitewater Affiliation (AWA), and the Southwestern classification of river difficulty. While these systems use different numerical ratings (the AWA scale uses a six-point system, and the Southwestern scale uses a ten-point system), they follow a similar progression. The International Scale is the most heavily used in this country.

The International Scale follows a progression from I to VI, with I being the easiest and VI being the most difficult. Here are the ratings:

Class I. Easy water. Not much gradient, with riffles and small waves. Wide, unobstructed channels.

Class II. Somewhat more difficult than Class I. Regular waves with relatively clear channels that require only occasional maneuvering.

Class III. Rapids of intermediate difficulty. Moderate, irregular waves that may be difficult to avoid. May require complex maneuvering. Scouting is advisable, especially if you've never seen these rapids before.

Class IV. For advanced paddlers. The rapids have big waves with many obstacles that require precise maneuvering in rough water. These rapids may have crux moves above dangerous obstacles.

Class V. For experts only. Long, violent rapids with dangerous obstructions. The consequences of an upset are likely to be dire, with long, dangerous swims with poor prospects for rescue.

Class VI. The limits of navigability. These are for the pros only, done only after close inspection, in favorable conditions, and with every possible precaution. For the purposes of this book, consider Class VI as unrunnable.

The Southwestern classification system, with its ten-point scale and a "U" for "unrunnable," correlates to the International Scale if you simply match two of the Southwestern scale's numbers to one of the International Scale's numbers.

The first thing you need to know about these rating systems is that they are highly subjective. One person's Class IV rapid is another person's Class II rapid. This subjectivity is compounded by the fact that a single river may be rated differently at different times of the year. On the lower Salmon River in Idaho there is a rapid that, at flows of 2,000 cfs, doesn't even exist. At 30,000 cfs (not an unusually high flow for the Salmon), it's considered a high Class V. And sometimes a river may become much more difficult to run at low flows because there are more obstacles.

Also, the International Scale doesn't describe the difficulty of big rivers really well. I once asked Bob Foote—well known for his many open canoe runs down the Grand Canyon—how he rated the Colorado through the Grand Canyon. He replied, "A big Class II." His rationale was that, while the waves are huge, they tend to be regular and the routes clear. On the other hand, even Bob agrees that the consequences of a long swim in those "big Class IIs" can be severe indeed.

So the bottom line is that, while these classification systems may give you some helpful first impressions about the difficulty of a piece of water, it's no substitute for the more precise descriptions of a good guidebook or the knowledge of experienced local river runners. When you head to a new river, get as much advance, local information as you can.

Chapter Three
Navigation

L et me make a disclaimer at the start of this chapter. This chapter is not a substitute for hands-on competent instruction. Instead, it should give you the basis for thinking about what you learn from those who teach you. That said, regardless of your craft—be it canoe, kayak, inflatable kayak, fixed-oar boat, or paddle raft—there are certain basic principles of navigation that apply. There are also specific navigation techniques that you should master in *any* craft.

At the outset, this suggests one thing, if nothing else. Learn how to use your craft. Ideally, you should find a course with qualified instructors to teach you. Failing that, find a skilled local boater and squeeze whatever knowledge you can out of that person. Remember that the huge majority of fatal accidents reviewed for this book involved people with no formal training in boat handling.

In any event, boating course or not, take your craft out on *still water*—a local swimming pool, pond, or lake— and learn to propel it. It's a profoundly bad idea to begin your learning process on moving water. The consequence of a mistake on still water is a dunking. The consequences of a mistake on moving water are usually more complicated than a simple dunking.

Practice moving your craft forward in a straight line, backward in a straight line, spinning it, and turning it. Practice these things until you have an intuitive sense of how the boat will respond to a given paddle or oar movement, so that when you're on the river, you don't have to think about the specific techniques you have to perform to make the boat go where you want. And practice your strokes using the safest posture or position for your boat. For example, in a paddle raft, practice with both legs *inside* the boat. while it may seem more comfortable to straddle the tubes, it is significantly more dangerous to have the leg dangling out there in busy water where it can get smashed or broken on rocks or other obstacles.

Muscle Groups

An important part of this learning process is to learn what muscles work best for making the boat respond. The conventional wisdom for all boats is that, as much as possible, you want to use the large muscle groups (abdominals, back, obliques) as opposed to the small muscle groups (arms).

For example, if you have a fixed-oar boat, you will make the boat respond more quickly if you pull on the oars instead of pushing on them. When you pull, you can use the muscles of the back and legs—instead of the smaller muscles of the arms that you push with. As a result, the conventional wisdom for rowers is to face the obstacle you want to avoid, so you can pull away from it. For you aspiring rowers out there, you can test this one on a pond by simply rowing forward (pushing) over a fixed distance against a clock, and then rowing backward (pulling) over the same distance. Which method moved you faster? Which method wore you down faster?

In various paddle craft, learn to use the oblique muscles (on most of us men, these are the ones that turn into "love handles" or, as I like to think of it, male cellulite) by using shoulder rotation to set up the stroke and to apply power to it.

On any boat, make sure you get your oar or paddle blade entirely in the water. You'll get much more out of your muscles if you bury that blade.

For every craft, there will be specific techniques for making optimal use of those muscle groups. The best place to learn those? From a qualified instructor.

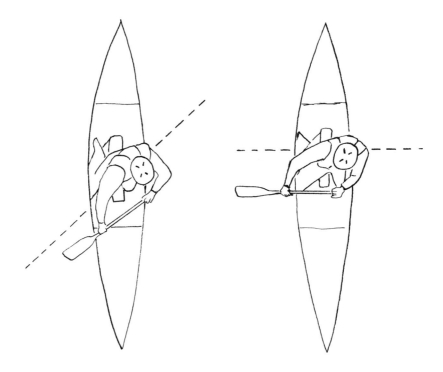

The key to a good paddle stroke is rotation at the waist. While the illustration is of a canoe, the principal is the same in kayaks and paddle rafts. Avoid the impulse to lean way forward and pull with your lower back muscles. It's not very efficient, and it will give you a sore back or worse.

Once you are comfortable moving your boat on still water, try your techniques on slow-moving water.

Cardinal Rules of Navigation

As we saw in Chapter One, a considerable percentage of accidents arise from a basic failure of common sense. The rules that follow in this chapter incorporate an understanding of river currents and common sense.

Respect inertia. *Webster's Collegiate Dictionary, Tenth Edition,* defines inertia: "A property of matter by which it remains at rest or in uniform motion in the same straight line unless acted upon in by some external force." For our purposes on the river, inertia means "an object in motion tends to remain in motion." In this case, the object is your boat, and you—with your oar or paddle—are the external force. So what does an axiom from eighth grade science class have to do with river running?

The next time you're on the water, try this little drill. Get some downstream momentum going—not a lot, just a little—and then let the boat drift for a while. After drifting a short way, pull hard on the oars or paddle to slow down in the current. Most of the time, on the first or second stroke, you'll feel as if you're trying to move the Empire State Building. The boat will respond little, if at all. It will take three or four strokes to slow or move the boat. Congratulations. You have just had a close encounter with inertia. So what?

One of the most common causes of river mishaps is the failure of the boater to react to a hazard until it is too late. Why? Because of inertia. When you see a hazard on the river that you want to avoid, get in the habit of taking a few strokes away from the hazard and toward your desired route *before* you think you need to. Break down the inertia of your boat and the current before it is too late. This leads us to the next basic rule.

Anticipate hazards by looking ahead. When in the midst of a float, whether on busy water or a lazy stretch, we often want to focus our gaze on the water right off our bow, at the spectacular scenery around us, or for us fly fishers, at our fly on the water—anywhere but downstream. If you are responsible for the navigation of your craft, get in the habit of moving your gaze from the edge of your boat to as far downstream as you can see—and then back to the more immediate navigational problems. Keep your eyes peeled ahead for potential hazards, shallows, bends in the river, and preferred routes. Watch an accomplished whitewater guide on a fixed-oar craft enter a rapid. She's likely to appear to be hardly working at all by the time she's in the rapid. That's because she anticipated and set up her route before she got there.

Anticipate your route. With a little practice, you'll find that this is not especially difficult. And it will go a long way toward saving you the grief of a mishap. Witness the consequences to my fly-fishing pals on Rock Creek.

Larry, Moe, and Curly Dodge a Bullet on Rock Creek

On a late June day in 1996, three fishermen floated Rock Creek east of Missoula. Rock Creek is famed for its trout fishery, and—especially in June—its salmon fly hatch. The salmon fly is named for its bright orange body—it's actually a stone fly. Big as your thumb and clumsy in flight, it drives fish—and consequently, fishermen—crazy.

Rock Creek is also steep, fast, riddled with sweepers, and an extremely busy stretch of water. On this particular day, the salmon flies were out and the fish were up. Larry and Moe are expert fly-fishermen and experienced oarsmen. Curly was somewhat new to fly-fishing and just learning how to row a raft. Most of the morning, Larry and Moe traded off at the oars while Curly fished. Finally, they let Curly take a turn at the oars. Given that bugs and fish were both active, Larry and Moe were soon intent on their fishing. So intent that they didn't see the logjam until it was too late.

As Larry describes it, the channel just above the logjam split to either side of an island. The logjam was in the left channel, But I'll let Larry tell it:

> The current split with most of it going to the left. We wanted to go down a small channel on the right. If it was a curve on a highway, we would have made it perfectly. Curly didn't know about the currents pulling to the left at the top of the split. The other bozos were in La-La Land.

By the time Larry and Moe realized what was happening, it was too late to take over the oars and pull the boat away. The boat slammed into the jam. Larry jumped towards shore; Moe and Curly went overboard and, with the boat, were immediately swept under the logjam. Here's the bottom side of a logjam in Moe's words:

> Once in the water, we went under the jam so fast I didn't have time to react. Before I knew it, I was banging into branches. It seemed like I was under there for hours. I was sure I was going to die. Amazingly, I popped out the other side. Curly came out just about the same time, We lost our boat and most of our fishing equipment, but, under the circumstances, we were lucky.

These anglers were indeed lucky, coming out of it with a big scare and some lost equipment.

Primary Factors Contributing to the Accident:

1. **Inappropriate training site.** First, Rock Creek—a fast, technical river in the spring and early summer—is not the place to train a novice rower. **Learn to handle your craft in easy, safe water where the consequences of mistakes are negligible.**

2. **Inadequate oversight by an experienced boater.** Second, even if Curly was ready to try more technical water, either Larry or Moe should have foregone the fishing to help Curly navigate and, if necessary, take over. **If you are teaching someone else on water that is at the limits of his skill, then work with him while he is rowing—to the exclusion of all else. Make sure you can take over, if necessary, to extricate the pupil from any potential problems.**

3. **Failure to anticipate the hazard.** Third, Curly either did not anticipate the hazard early enough and begin to set up for it, or he did not understand the current well enough to anticipate the problem. **Remember, look ahead and anticipate hazards before you get to them.**

Focus on where you want to go, not on what you want to avoid. A common downfall for many boaters is the tendency to fixate on the hazard they want to avoid. Too often they become so fixated that they don't plot their route to avoid the hazard. As a result, they plow right into the hazard. Once you identify your hazards, figure out the route to avoid them and then *concentrate on that route.*

Learn to use river currents and eddies to your advantage. One of the hardest ideas for many new boaters to grasp is the idea that we don't have to fight the river to navigate it. Our instinct is to view rocks only as obstacles, and current only as something to speed our descent to the take-out. Watch a really good boater move through a busy stretch of river. He or she will look effortless. They let the river do the work for them. As we will discuss in the next section, there are some basic navigational skills that you can use in *any* craft that will make the river feel like a much friendlier place.

Navigational Techniques

One of the first things to practice in your boat—no matter what kind of craft—is moving slower than the current. Don't forget that demon inertia. One of the best ways to counteract inertia is to maintain a steady—but easy—upstream propulsion by back-paddling or back-rowing. It is also the best way for slower craft—most canoes, rafts, and drift boats—to negotiate busy stretches of river. By moving the boat at something slower than current speed, you have more time to maneuver to avoid obstacles. Sounds simple, but the next time you're on a rough stretch of water, watch how many boaters break into a frenzied rush downstream. And watch how many things they hit and how wet they get. Not that getting wet is bad, but you should know how to stay dry; learning to control your boat by moving slower than the current is an important first step.

Ferries. A ferry uses the upstream momentum of the boat against the prevailing current to move the boat laterally from one place on the river to another. In principle, ferries are simple. In application—especially in paddle craft—it takes considerable practice to ferry a boat in complete control.

There are three elements to an effective ferry:
1. upstream boat momentum;
2. current speed; and
3. boat angle to the current.

Fixed-oar craft will usually ferry by pointing the stern of the boat upstream. Paddle craft can ferry by pointing either the bow or stern upstream. Paddlers, when your bow is upstream, it's a front ferry. When your stern is upstream, it's a back ferry.

To execute a ferry, align your boat at a slight angle (usually less than 45 degrees) to the current and propel the boat against the current. The slight angle exposes the side of the boat to the current enough to push the boat toward the bank at which the upstream end of the boat points without being swept downstream.

Practice your first ferries on slow-moving current. A good drill is to

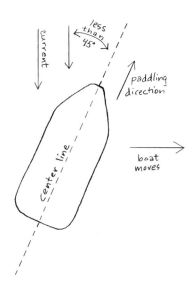

When you leave the eddy, start your ferry angle a little narrower than you think you need. This will keep the current from blowing you downstream. Once you have some upstream momentum, you can make whatever adjustments you need to cross the current efficiently.

pick out an obstacle on the far bank, either even with you (if you are in a canoe or kayak) or slightly below you (if you are in a raft or drift boat), and try to ferry across to it without getting swept below it. Two things you'll quickly learn:

1. Get too wide an angle to the current, and you'll get knocked sideways and spun downstream.

2. Get too narrow an angle, and your lateral movement across the stream is negligible.

Basic rule of thumb on ferries: The faster the current, the narrower your angle must be. Conversely, the slower the current, the wider your angle must be.

Another thing you will quickly notice; across any river, current speed usually changes several times. This means that you can't mindlessly set your angle and power away. If you do, you'll either find yourself stalled out and working your pants off (too little angle) or getting blown downriver (too much angle). Pay attention to the specific section of current you are on, not the general course of the river. A good ferry requires constant adjustment. Finally, when you get to the eddy at the end of your ferry, open the angle of your boat to the current slightly just before you cross the eddy line.

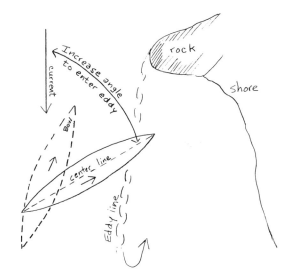

At the end of the ferry (in this case a forward ferry), widen your angle to break through the eddy line.

No sooner will you have read this section than you will go out to a river and see boaters speeding down the river, clearly in control, clearly skillful, with nary a ferry in sight. If you want to see really good boaters going really fast, go to a whitewater slalom race or a high-end marathon canoe race. So what is the point of ferries? It's simple. *Ferrying is the safest, most conservative way to move your craft down the river.* That does not mean that it is the only safe way. Once you have your ferries down cold, then you can experiment with the fast stuff. Under the guidance of an instructor ...

> **Ferries and Freight Boats**
> Ferries are essential for maneuvering heavily loaded craft through busy water. Watch the freight boats on any guided float trip. They tend to turn around and pull downstream through the open flats. At the rapids and rock gardens, they'll turn it back around and ferry through. Every once in a great while, you'll come upon a freighter mired on a rock or grounded on a sand bar. He probably forgot to ferry. Stop and give him a hand. He'll likely need it.

Eddies, sets, and turns. Eddies, those seeming calm spots downstream from rocks and inside bends (and almost any other obstacles), can be your best friends on a busy stretch of river. Remember, the water in that little patch of calm is actually moving upstream. If you can get your craft into it, you can rest, regroup, scout, and plot your route through the river below you. The trick is getting into them.

Setting into the eddy. Regardless of your craft, if you master your back ferry, you can "set" into an eddy. "Setting" is simply the act of back-ferrying to the inside of a bend or into an eddy. It's invaluable in a busy stretch of river; it can allow you the time to plot your course. Setting is especially valuable if you have a heavily loaded boat or kids aboard. If you learn your back ferries as described above, this is a relatively simple, but wonderfully elegant maneuver. The exhilaration of slipping into the quiet embrace of an eddy while the river rages around you is indescribable. Try it. You'll like it.

There are two primary things to practice to develop good, consistent sets:

1. Set into the eddy as close to the obstacle creating the eddy as possible. Ideally, you will clear the obstacle by inches. This puts the boat into the strongest part of the eddy current and reduces the chance of getting flushed out before you are ready to leave. If you hit too low in the eddy, you'll just flush out.

2. On the last stroke before entering the eddy, widen the boat's angle to the prevailing current. This will allow you to punch through the eddy

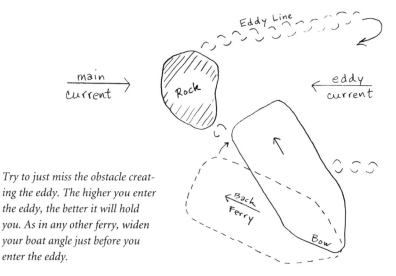

Try to just miss the obstacle creating the eddy. The higher you enter the eddy, the better it will hold you. As in any other ferry, widen your boat angle just before you enter the eddy.

line (or eddy "fence" in really fast water). The consequence of not open-
ing the boat angle will be that you simply slide helplessly by the eddy
instead of entering it. See the general discussion of ferries above.

Eddy-Hopping Practice

Setting will not come instantaneously. Find a relatively busy, but gentle, stretch to practice
on, and leave no eddy unset. Try setting on big eddies and little eddies (you'll be amazed at
how small an eddy will hold you). Above all, practice just clearing that rock, or stump, or point
that creates the eddy. At first, you'll spend a fair amount of time bouncing off the obstacle.
That's okay. That's how you learn to gauge your entry. With just a few days' practice, you'll be
dancing through stuff that stymied you before.

Eddy turns. An eddy turn entails moving your boat faster than the
prevailing current and crossing over the eddy line and into the eddy,
ending with the bow of your craft facing upstream. This maneuver is
most common to canoes and kayaks, but even paddle rafts and fixed-oar
craft can do eddy turns in a pinch.

An eddy turn uses the forces of two opposing currents to assist in
turning the craft. As the leading end of the craft crosses the eddy line,
the upstream current in the eddy pushes it upstream, while the river's
downstream current continues to push the trailing end of the boat
downstream. The effect of this action is to turn the boat into an
upstream/downstream alignment in the eddy.

Some basic considerations for the completion of an eddy turn:

1. You need enough forward momentum to drive the leading end of the
boat through the eddy line and into the eddy. If you don't have sufficient
speed, you'll just slide by the eddy (and maybe onto the nasty rock just
below it).

2. When the leading end of the boat crosses the eddy line, you want to
have the boat at well over a 45-degree angle to the eddy line and probably closer to 90 degrees. Without that angle, you again run the risk of
simply slipping by the eddy.

3. If you're in one of those "tippy" craft, such as a canoe or a kayak, you

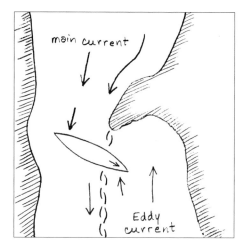

Boat angle is crucial to a successful eddy turn. If the angle is too narrow to the eddy line, you'll simply slip by the eddy without getting into it.

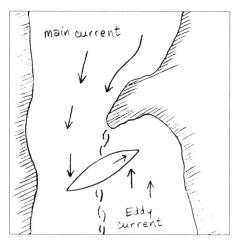

An eddy turn uses the force of opposing currents to turn the boat as you leave the main current and enter the eddy.

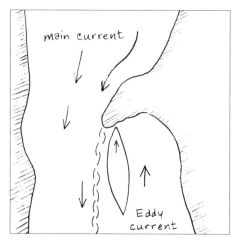

Once in the eddy and turned, move the boat close to the obstacle that caused the eddy. The eddy current will be strongest here.

want to tilt the boat in the direction of the turn, much as you lean a bicycle into the direction you are turning. If you don't, the upstream current of the eddy will push the bottom of the boat upstream and you'll find yourself leaning downstream—and then swimming and feeling stupid.

4. If you're in a paddle raft or fixed-oar craft, make sure you finish the turn with a few forward strokes toward the top of the eddy to offset any downstream momentum. Otherwise, the boat is liable to go right through the eddy and drift downstream, losing the benefits of the eddy turn.

Watch That Eddy Line

The eddy line only rarely aligns perfectly parallel to the primary course of the river. Often the obstacle creating the eddy causes the current to flair away from the obstacle at something approaching a 45-degree angle to the prevailing current. In this case, a 90-degree crossing of the eddy line will place your boat at approximately 45 degrees to the primary course of the river.

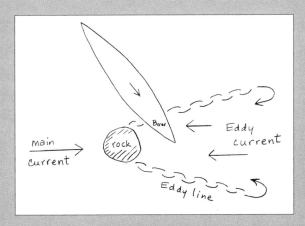

The moral? Pay attention to where the eddy line forms and how it presents itself to you.

The first time you pull off an eddy turn, it feels as if you've performed magic. All of a sudden, you've harnessed the power of the river and, instead of fighting it and inevitably losing—the strongest of us are still pretty puny when placed against the strength of even the smallest floatable river—you've gotten the river to work for you. Once you've figured

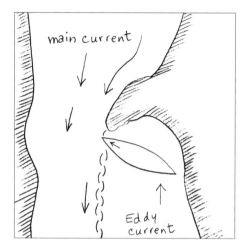

Peeling out gets you out of the eddy and back into the main current. Exit the eddy as close to the object creating it as possible.

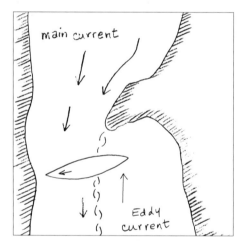

After the bow crosses the eddy line, turn the boat downstream into the main current. Remember, in canoes and kayaks, to "tilt" the boat downstream as you enter the main current, much as a bike rider would lean into a turn.

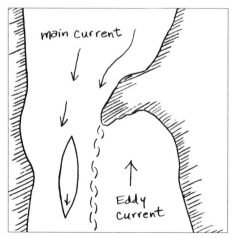

Your reward will be an upright boat continuing downstream.

out eddy turns, you'll find yourself seeking eddies to turn in, not because you have to, but just for the fun of it.

Peel-Outs. Once you have turned into an eddy and you're done basking in the glow of that perfect turn, you're going eventually have to leave the eddy. Peeling out is what you do when you leave an eddy. A peel-out is the mirror image of an eddy turn. You cross the eddy line as close as you can to the obstacle creating the eddy (unless you're in a hard-sided fixed-oar craft, of course), you try to hit the eddy line at close to 90 degrees, and, if you're in a "tippy" craft, tilt the boat in the direction you are turning.

Inside bends. Often, in a seriously meandering river with sharp bends that force the current directly into the outside bank at the end of the bend, the safest place you can be is on the inside of the bend. First, as previously discussed, the current below the point forming the inside bend will usually form an eddy. Lacking other options on a bad bend, perform an eddy turn or a set into the eddy on the inside of the bend, then exit out the bottom of the eddy.

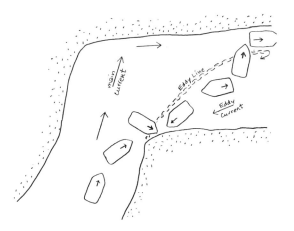

You can turn into the eddy on the inside bend of the river to avoid slamming into the bank on the out-side bend. You may have to work a little to get out the bottom of the eddy and back into the main current, but that is a small price to pay for not trashing your boat on the outside bank.

Another option for avoiding the outside bend is to back-ferry close to (but not across) the eddy line on the inside bend. If the river is wide enough, by maintaining your position on that eddy line you will get the benefit of downstream current without getting slammed into the outside bank. This move requires some precision; if you go too close to the inside bend, you'll get pulled into the eddy, and it will likely take some effort to get out. If you don't go close enough to the eddy line, you may get smacked into the outside bank anyway.

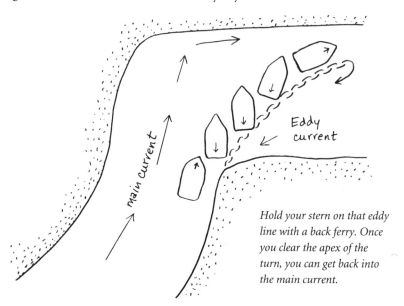

Hold your stern on that eddy line with a back ferry. Once you clear the apex of the turn, you can get back into the main current.

Scouting, lining, and portaging

Standard wisdom for running a rapid—or any other tough piece of water, for that matter—is "when in doubt, scout." Scout any rapid that the weakest or least experienced member of your party has any apprehension about. Scouting may not always be easy. Often the places that may seem the hairiest also have the steepest, roughest banks. Nonetheless, if you're not sure, scout it.

Scouting wisely. When you scout, follow these rules:

1. Go to the bottom of the reach you want to scout before beginning to scout.

2. Always select your route from the bottom of the reach to the top.

3. Find landmarks on the shore or in the river that you will be able to

see from the river to mark important moves or obstacles as you progress down the reach.

4. To the extent possible, as you move back up river while scouting, get down to water level and look back downstream from water level.

5. After you've decided if and how you'll run, line, or portage a rapid, go do it. After a while, looking at a rapid doesn't make it any harder or easier.

Go to the bottom of the rapid, and scout from the bottom to the top. Too often, it is sorely tempting to simply get up high, take a quick look at the most likely route, and jump in your boat and go. Don't. Instead, walk all the way. The only reliable way to plot a route through a complicated piece of water is to go to the bottom of the rapid and find your route in reverse. This way, you have the entire picture of the rapid.

As you identify key moves in your proposed route, find some landmark on shore, or in the river, that will help you orient yourself on the river so you will know when to make that move. It may be a distinctive rock or tree, or some big feature on the water, but find some milepost to mark those places where you have to make key moves. There is no worse feeling than, after having scouted a rapid, finding yourself on the water with no idea where to make your key move.

As you move back upriver while scouting, get down as close to water level as you can and look down your route. Rocks or other key obstacles or places on the river will look much different from downstream than they do from upstream. Rocks that seem huge when viewed from below may seem almost invisible when viewed from above. Also, remember, when you are in your boat, your head may be only a couple of feet or so above water level. Those obstacles will look much different from water level than they do when you look down on them from fifteen feet up on the riverbank.

If you don't think you can handle a particular stretch of river, portage it or line it. *Do not let others pressure you into doing something you're not ready for.* If you haven't run into him already, sooner or later you'll run into some macho slackjaw who will try to bully you into doing

This is the view of Salmon River's Pine Creek Rapid from the bridge.

This is the water-level view of Pine Creek at the entry. The slight bend in the river at the bridge hides most of this rapid until you are in the thick of it. The moral? Scout it.

something you're not ready for. Or he may try to pressure you into doing something foolhardy. There is no shame in saying, "I can't do this." And don't let anyone tell you otherwise. The decision to run or not to run a particular piece of water is highly personal, and no responsible boater will try to browbeat you into doing something you don't think you can handle. The boater who does try to push you into such a position is an idiot and deserves only your scorn (and maybe a swift kick in the slats).

Lining and portaging. Lining a boat down the river entails attaching floating lines to the bow and stern of the boat and guiding it down the edge of the river from shore. It is crucial to use floating lines (woven polypropylene) and to have enough line to move the boat laterally from side to side. A good rule of thumb is to have two lines, each of which is at least one and one-half times the length of your boat. If you expect to do a lot of lining, take even longer lines. Tie in your gear securely if you line your boat. A couple of cautionary notes—wear your PFD while lining, and if you have to wade, wade with caution. The point here is to stay out of trouble.

If a reach is too dangerous or difficult to line, then you'll have to portage. When you portage your boat, you take it out of the water and carry it downstream. You aren't likely to view portaging as the apex of the river-running experience, especially if you have to portage a raft or a lot of gear. On the other hand, if the alternative is an ugly wreck with serious injury or even death in the balance, then a portage doesn't sound like such a bad deal. One suggestion—scout your portage route *before* you start down it. A check of the easiest route may save you considerable grief and exertion.

> **Preplanning a Rescue**
> When members of your party decide to run a rapid that pushes the limits of their ability, set up a rescue downstream by sending a more experienced boat down first, to wait at the bottom of the rapid. If you have enough people and the rapid is long, deploy people along the shore with throw ropes (see Chapter Four, The Basics of River Rescue, for a detailed discussion of throw ropes).

Coping with Wind

In 1988, several other guides and I were guiding a group of anglers on the Blackfoot River in western Montana. We were in fixed-oar rafts. When we started our trip, it was a little overcast, but calm and pleasantly cool for a midsummer day. A mile down river, in the course of about five minutes, a wind storm blew in from downstream, tearing the tops off waves and creating waves where none had been. With the wind came a ferocious lightning storm. Being a notorious sissy about lightning, I wrestled our boat to shore at a grove of low lying willow bushes. It was just as well. It was all I could do to make any forward progress.

My guiding buddy Jon was more determined. As he pulled abreast of my spot on shore, I yelled at him to come on in. He pointedly ignored me and leaned harder into the oars. Five minutes later, and ten feet further down stream, he finally gave it up, and let the wind blow him to shore. He no sooner got hunkered under the willows with us than the storm really opened up. Old cottonwoods on the opposite bank started crashing to the ground, and the storm intensified until the willows flattened over us like a blanket. Twenty minutes later, the storm passed and the sun came out. That's typical river weather.

Sooner or later we all encounter the killer wind on the stream. If it's bad enough, like our day on the Blackfoot, the only sane thing to do is to get off the water until it passes.

Often, however, the wind won't be that bad, but just bad enough to be really annoying and disruptive to your navigation. The problems posed by the wind change according to its direction. If it's coming at your back from upstream, you may simply have to back ferry some to counteract its effect. If it comes from downstream, you may have to start actively rowing or paddling downstream to counteract its effects. As Jon's experience illustrates, a strong wind from downstream can stop you cold, even in a strong current.

The most difficult to deal with are winds that blow laterally. These winds may require you to perform a radical ferry to simply keep your line, or to even abandon the ferry and to aggressively row or paddle lateral to the primary direction of the current. When this happens, the rule about anticipating what's ahead becomes even more important. Once you've abandoned your ferry, your progress downstream may increase, reducing your reaction time to hazards ahead. One tactic to reduce the effects of the wind is to move closer to the side of the river from which the wind is coming. This can give you some shelter in the lee of the river bank. Of course it only works if the route on that side of the river doesn't take you into other hazards.

In some instances, if the direction of the wind is relatively consistent, either upstream or down, you can use it to assist your ferry. After all, the wind is a form of current—just in a different medium. Set your angle and drive into the wind and ferry on it.

But if it's too bad to safely manage, get off the water and wait it out.

Chapter Four
The Basics of River Rescue

R iver rescue" conjures up images of helicopters, big jet boats, and
other tools of our highly technical, motorized existence all converging to snatch the hapless victim from a rock in the middle
of a wild and deadly torrent. At least that's what usually shows up on
television. Most of the rescue situations you encounter in boating will
be much less dramatic. In fact, most of your rescues will likely be self-
rescues. Occasionally, you may find yourself either the recipient of or
a participant in an assisted rescue, where the worst consequence is a
wrecked boat or some wrecked equipment. If you're lucky, that's as
bad as it will get.

This chapter—like the last one on navigation—is simply an intro-
duction to some basic river rescue techniques that should be in every
floater's bag of skills. It is *not* the comprehensive compendium of every-
thing-you-ever-need-to-know-about-river-rescue. Take a course—several
courses—for that. Nonetheless, pay attention to the information in this
chapter. It may save your life.

In either kind of rescue—self- or assisted—remember this cardinal
rule and follow it: **people first, and boats and equipment second.**
Often, if you can stay with your boat, it will help keep you afloat. But if
staying with your boat puts you in greater peril, abandon it.

A Close Call on the Sun

In mid-May 1989, during a canoe instructor's class on the Sun River, Bruce and Diane—both strong paddlers— flipped while practicing ferries in a strong jet of current. Bruce set out for shore shortly after the capsize, dealing with his own problems from a too-loose vest (see Chapter One). He made it to shore relatively quickly. Diane, proud owner of the brand-new boat in which they flipped, elected to stay with the boat and attempt to get both herself and the boat to shore.

At high water, the reach of the Sun where the accident happened is continuous whitewater for about a half mile. It was a balmy spring day, but the water temperature was in the mid-40 degree F range. Diane had neither a dry suit nor a wet suit, but was layered in polypropylene clothes. As she floated downriver with the boat she got in the proper position upstream of the boat, and managed to fend off rocks in the rapid. Diane bounced down several hundred yards of whitewater before she was able to reach shore.

By the time she reached shore, she was too cold and weak to pull herself out of the water. Fortunately, several of us had chased after her along the bank and were able to pull her out within a minute or so after she hit the shore. A few minutes in the warm May sun, and she mostly recovered. Had she gone much farther, or had she not gotten help out of the water, she might easily have succumbed to hypothermia.

Primary Factor Contributing to the Accident:

Leaning upstream. The cause of the accident was fairly straightforward. The paddlers leaned upstream coming out of an eddy and into the current and flipped. See Chapter Two sidebar, "That Demon Upstream Lean," and Chapter Three, Navigation.

Primary Factor Contributing to Diane's Close Call:

Failure to follow basic rule. First, Diane disobeyed the cardinal rule. A skilled, seasoned, and extremely safety-conscious paddler and an experienced Red Cross instructor, Diane knew the proper progression—people first, boats and equipment second. If the water had been warmer and perhaps a little less pushy, her decision to stay with the boat might not have had such dire consequences.

In the grip of cold spring runoff, however, she quickly lost strength. This was exacerbated by her lack of a wet suit or dry suit. But let Diane tell it:

I realized that I could not get the boat to shore, especially without Bruce's assistance. As I bounced down the river, I could see that I was headed for a narrow chute stuffed with a large boulder and a train of standing waves. That's when I decided to abandon the boat. But by then, the cold had already taken its toll. I should have made for shore earlier while I still had the strength to do it.

With the aid of a wet suit or dry suit, her ordeal might have been considerably less harrowing.

A postscript to that close call on the Sun: Later that day, the same brand-new boat—different paddlers—flipped again in the same spot. This time, we had rope throwers lined along the bank below the exercise. Both paddlers went for the ropes and let the boat go. The boat then continued down about a half mile of heavy rapids and settled out a mile or so below the mishap on a logjam in an irrigation reservoir. It was nearly broken in half, held together by a thin strip of Royalex directly below the rear seat. However, with the help of a roll of trusty duct tape (see Appendix C, The Basic Dry Bag) and some sticks, we were able to patch it up and paddle it out to the road. The paddlers escaped without a scratch.

Remember the cardinal rule: **Protect yourself first, then worry about your equipment.**

If you are the rescuer, remember **Cardinal Rule Number Two: Never put yourself at risk in the course of rescuing another.** Don't make the situation worse by adding yourself to the list of victims. And remember **Cardinal Rule Number Three: Never put anyone else at risk in the name of performing a rescue.**

Self-rescue

If you upset in your boat, your most obvious source of rescue is close at hand. It's you.

Cardinal Rules for Self-rescue
1. Wear your PFD.

2. Once you are in the water, get upstream of your boat. The pounds per square inch that river current exerts on the hull of a boat are enormous. If you happen to be between your boat and a hard spot when they collide, the current will trap you—and may crush you.

3. Where feasible, swim aggressively toward shore. Unless you are in a rocky, shallow stretch of water, swim aggressively toward safety. Among other techniques, you can ferry across the current in the same fashion that you would in a boat. See Chapter Three, Navigation, for a detailed discussion of ferrying.

If you find yourself in rocky, shallow water, roll over onto your back with your head upstream, keep your butt as near the surface as you can, and use back strokes to ferry and maneuver. Use your feet to fend off rocks and other obstacles.

current

Use the defensive swimming position to get through rocky, shallow water. When you're clear of the rocks, swim aggressively for shore.

In waves, time your breathing to inhale in the troughs and turn your head sideways to the current as you inhale. It is possible to get disoriented and inhale as the wave hits you in the face. If you find yourself in that sequence, change the timing of your breathing to inhale in the trough.

4. Swim into the shallows. Do not attempt to stand up in the river until the water level is below your knees. Remember the force of that current. If you attempt to wade in deep, moving water after an upset, you risk foot entrapment (your foot getting wedged between rocks) and pinning. A number of people have drowned when they attempted to stand up in fast water while swimming. Doing this is particularly dangerous in the eastern United States, where there is an abundance of undercut rocks and ledges.

5. If you can safely reenter your craft after a capsize, do it. As a rule, you will be safer in your boat than swimming, even if your boat is full of water. But remember, don't try to reenter from the downstream side.

6. If you are in the water and you cannot avoid a strainer, swim aggressively to it and pull yourself up on the strainer.

7. If you get trapped in a hole, try to relax and not fight the current. I know, this sounds like one of those impossible instructions—the hole is trying to drown you and you're supposed to relax. Right . . . but, if you recall the description of holes in Chapter Two, Reading the Water, a hole has a distinct recirculating current. You need to use that recirculation. Rather than fight it, try to go with the current and flush out the side or bottom.

Also, the more surface area a hole has to work with, the more control it can exert on you. So let go of your boat and pull yourself into as tight a ball as you can. Changing into this more compact shape may help you in flushing out the side of the hole.

8. If you drop over a ledge, pull your feet up. A ledge drop can be another source of foot pins. Better to take a bruising on your butt and clear the ledge than to risk a foot pin.

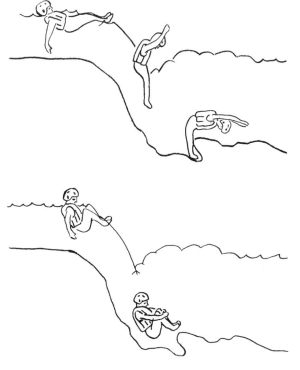

If you drop over a ledge, don't keep your feet extended; you'll risk a foot pin. Instead, pull your feet up and keep them close to your body.

9. If you capsize in rough water and you have companions on shore, look for them. They may be trying to toss you a rescue rope. This may seem self evident in the warmth of your study as you read this, but when you're in the middle of a nasty wave train, it's not that hard to forget this one. Don't. A good rope rescue can shorten your swim significantly.

Assisted Rescue

River rescue can be as simple as reaching down and pulling someone from the water with your hand or a paddle or a stick. Or it can be so complex as to require a trained team of rescuers with specialized equipment. We will focus on the simplest, most expedient methods. If you want to learn more sophisticated rescue methods, there are many good courses around the country and a number of good books and videos specifically on the topic. In the back of this book, see the Bibliography and Appendix F, Directory of Schools and Organizations, for references.

Cardinal Rules for Assisted Rescue

1. Don't put yourself or others at risk—attend to your own safety first, then those with you in your party, and then to the victim. All too often the temptation in a rescue situation is to do just about anything to complete a rescue, including life-endangering swims or wades. Remember, if you manage to get yourself into trouble, then you've only worsened the other victim's chances for a safe rescue (now that you're a victim, too). Second, make sure that others near the scene are safe, and don't do anything to endanger them.

2. Remember this sequence of rescue methods—reach, throw, row, go. These four words describe the hierarchy of methods—from the most desirable to the least desirable— that you should consider at the outset of a rescue. First, if you can simply reach out with a paddle or a hand and pull someone to shore, do it. If they are too far out for that, use a throw bag (see below). If they get beyond the range of a throw rope, get in your boat and go after them (if you are already in your boat, this may be your first option). As a last resort, you may have to swim or wade to someone's rescue. Swim or wade only if you cannot do one of the other three methods, only if you have some assistance to lessen the risk (see assisted swimming or wading below), and only if it is safe. A swimming rescue in rough water (or even slow-moving water, for that matter) is brutally difficult.

3. Buy a throw bag, learn to throw it, and *always* **have one in your boat.** If you spend a lot of time on rivers, you'll eventually have occasion to use your throw rope. If you don't know how to use it, the chances are good that you'll blow it when your moment arrives. A throw rope is not difficult to use, but it takes some practice to get reasonably accurate and reliable with it.

Practice, Practice, Practice!

With some practice, a throw bag can be your best friend on the river. Without any practice, it's just another piece of gear cluttering up your boat. But how to practice? Most of us don't live on a stream where we can practice throwing regularly. Besides, what a pain to have to repack your throw bag every time you throw it. Not to worry. Practice is as near as your local park or municipal playing field.

Here's the drill. Go to your local park or ball field with your throw bag and a partner. Start about fifteen feet apart. Leave the rope in the bag. Toss it to your partner. Practice lobbing it toward her head. Try overhand and underhand until you find one method that you like best. After a few warm-up throws, move farther apart and take a few more throws. Keep widening the gap until you can't reach each other, or until you're about fifty to sixty feet apart. (Most throw ropes are sixty-five feet long or less, and as you'll likely notice, most people can't throw much past that anyway.) Once you find your maximum distance, move a few feet closer to your partner.

Now start throwing to a moving target. As your catcher starts to move, try throwing the bag to her without having it land in front or in back of her.

Do these drills for ten or fifteen minutes a couple of nights a week for a few weeks, and you'll be able to nail your throws on the river. After the first couple of times, all the other people at the park will get used to the weirdos with the bag . . .

A second—and even more valuable—suggestion: On one of those hot days on the river, do a little throw-rope practice at a lunch break. Have people float down to you in a gentle current (pick a place where their swim to shore won't trash them on rocks or in a hole) and practice throwing the bag to them. This is a little different from the ball field, and it's a great way to get some practice while having a little fun. An added benefit—it assures that your floating pals get some practice. After all, you want them to nail you with the throw bag when you need it.

The most common materials for a throw rope—as of this writing—are ⅜-inch or ½-inch polypropylene or Spectra. Both are soft, floating ropes. If you decide to make your own throw rope, make sure you use one of these two materials. A sinking throw rope is almost worse than no rope at all. **Caution: Don't make too long a throw rope.** The weight of a seventy-five-foot throw rope can make it exceedingly difficult to throw. Sixty-five feet is as much as most people can throw.

Between polypropylene and Spectra, Spectra is the stronger of the two ropes. It is also much less elastic than polypropylene. These characteristics make it better for use in situations requiring the use of some mechanical advantage. It is also about twice as expensive as polypropylene. On the other hand, polypropylene works just fine for rescuing swimmers.

Whatever kind of throw bag you get, don't scrimp. There are some really cheap models with small tightly packed bags and cheap rope that won't throw well and are hard to repack. Stay away from these. Make sure the bag is big enough to easily repack.

Throw-rope technique—the thrower's job: There are a few basic things you need to know for an effective throw-rope rescue:

    a. First, find a place from which to throw that allows you to brace with your feet. Once, while practicing my throw-rope technique on the lower Salmon, I stood on a small pedestal of rock to perform a throw. The throw was good, but when Sue hit the end of the rope, I was airborne. Fortunately I went into a deep eddy, the air temperature was 100 degrees F that day, and I needed a swim. But the lesson was a graphic one. Get braced and stable when making your throw. When possible, have a second person anchor you by grabbing the shoulders of your PFD and leaning and pulling as the swimmer starts to swing to shore.

    b. Open the bag and pull out a couple of feet of rope.

    c. Always keep the end of the rope in your non-throwing hand. This is critical. Once, during a rescue class on the upper Gallatin in early June, I was on the receiving end of a throw that did not heed this rule. We were practicing throw ropes at the base of a Class II–III rapid. I was one of the designated victims. The instructor had suggested that the throwers place the end of the rope under one foot as an additional assurance of stability. When my rescuer made his throw, he started with the end of the rope under his foot. His throw was right on the money.

But the momentum of his throw caused him to lift his foot—and he hadn't held on to the end of the rope. It took me about fifty feet before I realized that it was just the rope and me out there all by ourselves. There's nothing quite so discouraging as hanging on to a throw rope without a rescuer on the other end. One caution here, thrower—*do not* wrap the rope around your hand so that you can't let go. If you get pulled in, you're just another victim. But please, at least hang onto the rope when you throw it.

d. Yell "Rope" to the victim. If the swimmer doesn't know the rope is coming, he may miss it. Yell "Rope" until you get some indication that the swimmer hears you. Jump up and down, if necessary, to get the victim's attention.

e. Throw the rope using either an underhand toss or an overhand throw. Aim your throw directly at and slightly past the victim. Whichever of these two methods you use—underhand or overhand—make sure that you move your throwing arm directly forward. Sidearm throws are usually a disaster.

Practice swinging your arm directly back-to-front. Even the slightest amount of sidearm action can make it much more difficult to throw accurately.

Aim your throw right at the swimmer. If you have to err, throw a little long. A rope that lands just two feet short is a rope that the swimmer probably won't reach. The second the rope hits short, the current starts pulling it downstream and toward shore. It's almost impossible for the swimmer to get to it before it swings out of reach. The same goes for a downstream throw. If you have to err upstream or down (and with practice, you shouldn't have to err), err to the upstream side of the swimmer. Then the swimmer has at least a chance to reach the rope with a ferrying stroke.

f. Once the swimmer has the rope, get braced and let him swing into shore, looking downstream to make sure that the swimmer will be able to safely get to shore. If the swing of the rope brings the swimmer into the wrong place, you may have increased your problems. If necessary, move downstream so the swimmer comes into a safe place.

Throw-rope technique—the swimmer's job. Throw-rope rescues require some teamwork between the swimmer and the thrower. If you are the swimmer, regardless of your personal strategy for self-rescue, look to shore to locate potential rescuers—especially the ones with the throw rope.

When the rescuer makes the throw, grab the rope while turning your back *toward* your rescuer. (Note: Don't try to grab the bag unless that is all you can reach. If you have the bag, you drift a lot farther before the rope swings you to shore. If you grab the rope where it lands on you, you'll get to shore much faster.) Hug the rope into your chest so that it runs over your shoulder to the rescuer.

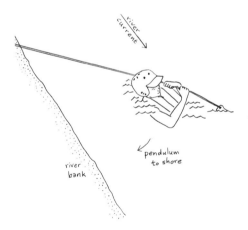

You may hear some debate about whether the rope should come over the shoulder closest to the rescuer or furthest from the rescuer. Either way will work, although away from the rescuer sets a little better angle for the swing into shore. If someone throws you a rope and you really need it, don't waste a lot of time worrying about which shoulder you put the rope on. Worry about it in your practice sessions. Most important is to turn your back to the rescuer so the pull of the rope does not bury your face in the water.

4. If you are rescuing from your boat, make sure that you don't endanger yourself or anyone else in attempting to get to the swimmer. Depending on your craft and the water conditions, you may be able to rescue the boat and the boater, getting both back on the water without ever going to shore. This is especially true if you're performing the rescue from a raft. Make sure, however, that you don't put the swimmer between your boat and a hard spot. Again, a boat and a rock with a swimmer between them, and even a moderate current, can squish that swimmer like a grape. So *always* pay attention to your position in relation to the swimmer and any other obstacles on the river.

Boat-bumping Rescues
    A hard-sided boat such as a canoe or kayak can help a swimmer get a boat to shore by bumping it as the swimmer pulls it.

If you are in a hard-sided boat, you can help a swimmer get a boat—even a raft—to shore by bumping it toward the bank. It's not especially speedy, but it is a big help to the swimmer trying to get the boat to shore.

More Tips for Assisted Rescues

Lifting a swimmer into a raft or canoe. Both rafts and canoes present their own challenges when you're pulling someone into them—rafts because they have large tubes that make it hard to get a purchase on the swimmer, and canoes because they tend to be unstable when you're pulling someone over the gunwale. Neither is impossible.

In a raft, brace your knees against the tube above the swimmer and grasp the shoulders of her life jacket. Keeping your back straight, stand up and lean back toward the opposite tube until you're able to sit down on it.

This is a move that can be extremely unfriendly to your back if you are careless about it. Make sure you lift with your legs, and not your lower back. Once the victim's torso has cleared the tube, just fall back toward the opposite tube.

In a canoe, turn the swimmer so his back is to you (or have the swimmer turn himself), then reach under his right arm and across to grab his left wrist. Do the same with his left arm and right wrist. Then stand and pull and lift the swimmer into your boat. One helpful suggestion: Make sure the victim's PFD will clear the gunwale. This will work best if you have another boat (i.e. the victim's boat) to place over your canoe like an outrigger. This isn't the most stable of rescues, but it may be all you have. Practice this one in the local pond on a hot summer day.

In a canoe, use this technique only if you don't have any other option and you have to get the victim in the boat. If you have another boat or another swimmer to stabilize you, use the boat as an outrigger or the other swimmer to counterbalance your lift.

Quick stabilization of a trapped victim. When a victim suffers from a foot entrapment or is pinned on a strainer, it is important to stabilize that person so that he or she doesn't get into a worse predicament while you are trying to complete the rescue. In many cases, this simply entails setting up a line down current from the victim, then running it back to the victim, and setting it at chest height to hold the victim's head above water.

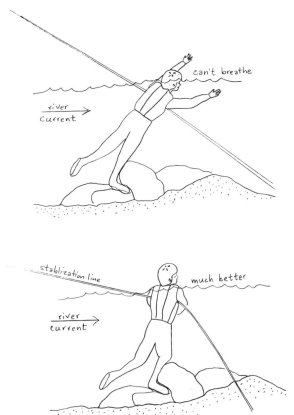

A stabilization line can keep a trapped victim alive until you can extricate him. If you have to run a line, be sure to place somebody upstream to warn floaters coming into the area so they don't complicate your rescue or endanger themselves. Also, make sure one side of the line can be quickly released, if necessary, to avoid snagging other people on the line.

To set up a stabilization line, run a line across the river downstream of the victim. Secure it at both ends, but be sure to have one end that you can easily release into the river in case the victim breaks loose. (See the sidebar below, Running Lines Across the River). Make sure the people belaying the line are set before bringing the line up to the victim. Then slowly move the line to within the victim's reach. Try to get the line about halfway up the victim's trunk, just under the armpits.

The stabilization line may provide the victim enough stability to extricate himself from the pin. But that's not its primary purpose. It buys you time to get the victim out alive. Once a victim is stabilized, you can run a second line, called a snag line, to the victim, work it down to where the foot is trapped, and use it to free the foot by pulling upstream. There is an excellent demonstraton of this in the video, *Heads Up: River Rescue for River Runners.* See the Bibliography.

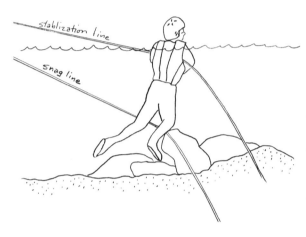

A snag line can be used to free a trapped foot or leg by getting the line down as close to the entrapment as you can and pulling upstream.

Swimming rescue. The simplest rule on swimming rescues is *don't.* Swimming rescues are extremely difficult and dangerous. Advanced rescue classes practice swimming rescues, in part, to illustrate just how difficult they are. If you doubt that, try swimming out and towing in a friend in a calm, safe, slow-moving stretch. Then try it with your friend resisting some. Then imagine doing it in a Class III rapid. It's extremely tough duty.

A group of people, wading as a unit, can wade difficult water much more safely than a solo wader.

If you have no option but to go after a person without the aid of a boat, consider wading with the support of a stabilization line, a paddle, or other waders.

Running Lines across the River

With the exception of the stabilization line described previously, if you must run a line across the river, never run it perpendicular to the current. A perpendicular line can snag rescuers or bystanders who may float into it, without offering any way of escape. Run a line 30 to 45 degrees to the current direction. This will allow a person on the line to slide toward the bank on the downstream end of the line. Again, with the stabilization line, make sure one end can be quickly released.

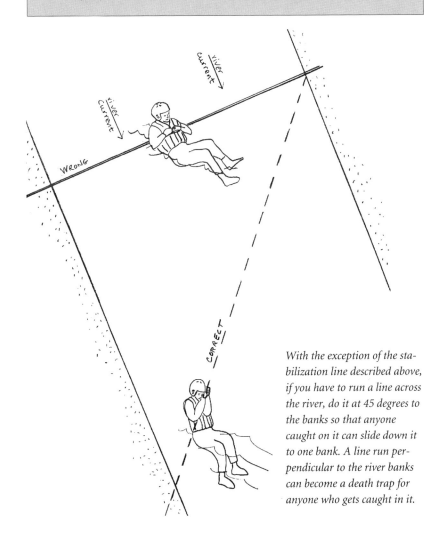

With the exception of the stabilization line described above, if you have to run a line across the river, do it at 45 degrees to the banks so that anyone caught on it can slide down it to one bank. A line run perpendicular to the river banks can become a death trap for anyone who gets caught in it.

Unwrapping a boat. As with other aspects of rescue, the simplest method is usually the best. If you can muscle a boat off an obstacle without a line, great. Do it. You may find, however, that it will take more than a little brute force and ignorance. If so, your next step is to use a line and as many strong bodies as you can muster. If that doesn't work, there are a number of leverage advantages that you can rig. Appendix G, Knots and Mechanical Advantage, describes these riggings and suggests the equipment necessary to do them. There are a number of other references cited in the Bibliography that provide in-depth explanation of these lever systems and how to use them.

> Caution!
> A pinned boat is just another strainer. Never approach a pinned boat from upstream. Always approach it from downstream. Try to avoid being where the boat can pin you if it breaks loose. Sounds like a tall order. Following a few basic rules can reduce the risk of working on a pinned boat:
> 1. Plan an escape route in case the boat shifts. Remember, never put yourself or others at risk to rescue people or equipment.
> 2. Keep one hand on the boat so that you are immediately aware of any movement by the boat.
> 3. Avoid placing any part of your body into gaps between the boat and rocks.

Theories of release on three kinds of boat pins. There are basically three kinds of boat pins:

center pin

A center pin can wrap the boat around the obstacle.

end-to-end pin

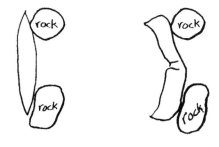

The current flowing in a center-pinned boat can fold it in half.

and **vertical pin**

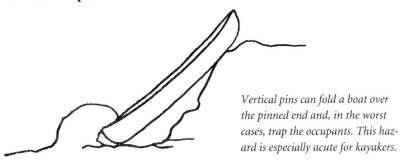

Vertical pins can fold a boat over the pinned end and, in the worst cases, trap the occupants. This hazard is especially acute for kayakers.

For each of these pins, there is a basic approach that will get the boat free in most cases:

Center pin. Usually, center pins are not "dead center" pins. One end of the boat is likely to be closer to the obstacle than the other, or one end is likely to be more out of the water than the other. Work on the end that is closest to the obstacle or most out of the water, and try to unbalance the pin to the point where the end most exposed to the current catches enough leverage to pull the boat off the pin. Remember, the force of the current on the hull of the boat is huge. Lifting one end up and out of the water will be easier than trying to pull one end straight back against the current. Again, if you can free it without having to rig a line, that's your best option.

End-to-end pin. On an end-to-end pin, your best option is to free one end by lifting it up and over the obstacle. The biggest threat in an end-to-end pin is that the boat (or in the case of rafts, the rowing frame) folds in half in the middle. Suffice it to say, time is of essence to keep your boat or rowing frame from turning into a pretzel.

Vertical pin. Vertical pins usually occur with hard-sided boats like canoes and kayaks. These are often the most dangerous boat pins—because they are unstable. With the advent of progressively more difficult kayak maneuvers, vertical pins all too often involve a trapped paddler, especially in the eastern United States, where there is an abundance of undercut rocks and ledges. In these cases, it is important to stabilize the boat quickly. If the boat shifts while you are working to release it, the shift usually makes it harder to extricate. Often your best option for releasing this pin is to pull the boat back upstream. This isn't easy.

The Risk of Breaking Lines

If you're using a stretchy line such as polypropylene or nylon to pull a boat off an obstacle, place a life preserver on the line a few feet from the boat. Then, if the line breaks loose (failed carabiner, broken boat part), the line and whatever projectile it still carries will fall harmlessly into the water instead of slingshotting and bonking the person pulling on the other end of the rope.

CHAPTER FIVE

TRIP ORGANIZATION AND RIVER COMMUNICATION

Getting Ready for the Trip

One really simple way to optimize your chances for a safe outing on the river is to engage in some basic pretrip planning. This should happen regardless of whether it's a half-day trip on your local stream or a three-week expedition in the Arctic. The level of detail and intensity for the two may be different, but both trips require forethought. Now, for a lot of you, this may seem like such basic common sense that, as you read this you're thinking, "Duh . . . some real river wisdom. I paid how much for this book? When do we get to the good stuff?" To which I can only say, it's all good.

Astoundingly enough, not everyone is as organized as you and me. You want proof? The next time you go on a river trip where lots of people are along (especially if there are people new to you on the trip), check how many people brought basic stuff like rain gear, PFDs (that's right—PFDs—you'd be amazed), or drinking water. Pretty basic stuff, but stuff that routinely gets ignored or forgotten. That's basic planning.

A good place to start is with the dry bag list in Appendix C. If you check that against what everyone in your group has before you start, then pass go and collect $200. Or at least get in your car and drive to the river.

Trip planning involves more that just equipment. If you're the organizer (or leader) of the trip, critically assess the skills of the people going on the trip and choose a route that everyone in the group can handle. **The capacity of the least skilled person in the group should dictate the water and route chosen. Do not place people in danger by placing them on water they are not ready for.**

Get some idea of the physical condition of the people in your group, make sure you know of any special medical conditions among the group's members, and factor that into your choice of water (e.g., are there any non-swimmers in the group?). If so, you might want to pick a relatively mellow trip that minimizes the chances of a hairy swim. Again, pick a trip that you know everyone in the group can handle.

If you're going to new water, gather as much intelligence about the water *before* you get there—maps, guidebooks, or personal knowledge of local paddlers.

Before you head out, let someone staying behind know your intended route and your expected return time. More than one floater has had his fat pulled out of the fire when someone at home said "Where the heck *are* they?"

Group Dynamics On the Water

Once you get to the river, a little basic organization is a good thing. You, as the trip organizer, should take the lead. On the other hand, if the trip organizer appears to be out in space, you—as the sole source of wisdom in your group—should adroitly and diplomatically take charge. Make sure everyone knows the same river signals. Identify a lead boat and a sweep boat (the most experienced boats).

The Safety Talk

Discuss some basic safety procedures. Make sure everyone knows what to do in case of an upset. If you have some relatively inexperienced boaters along, or you're not sure of the experience level in your group, discuss the basics of self-rescue, such as getting upstream of the boat, river signals, and the priorities of self-rescue. Discuss how to get somebody back in the boat in the case of an upset. If necessary, demonstrate it. If you plan a stop, set a time and stick to it. Don't assume knowledge among your partners in the group. After all, if you get in trouble, you want to know that they can help you.

If you have a group of paddle rafters along who haven't boated together before, make sure that each boat has a "captain" in the stern who can conduct the navigation, and make sure they all understand the basic navigational commands (e.g. "all forward," "all back," "right back," "left back," "stop," "high side").

Once on the water, the lead and sweep boats should make sure that one boat is always within sight of another boat. This doesn't mean that, in a large group, every boat should be able to see every other boat, but there should always be some visual contact between each boat and at least one other boat. The lead boat has the responsibility for judging the best route (keeping in mind the abilities of the weakest paddler), determining which rapids to scout and generally anticipating what is ahead, and, when necessary, pulling the group to shore to scout or portage questionable water. The sweep boat must keep track of everybody, and make sure that there are no stragglers.

So what is the optimal safe group size on a river trip? This is a question fraught with dissension among experienced floaters. Strictly speaking, if you want to optimize the safety of your trip, try to have at least three boats. This may vary according to the difficulty of the water. On a bathtub-flat, slowly moving river with little in the way of objective hazard, two may be plenty. If you're running whitewater, three is the *minimum*. Beyond six or seven boats, you may find the group size becomes unwieldy.

What About Solo?

One of the most problematic issues in river safety revolves around the growing appeal of the solo trip. There is a great feeling of independence and freedom that can attend a solo trip. As one who has taken a number of solo trips and who spends a fair amount of time on the water alone during my daily paddling on the local pond, I'm hardly in a position to say, "Don't do it." So I won't say that.

Nonetheless, if you contemplate a solo trip, carefully consider the consequences of an upset or injury, and plan your trip accordingly. Remember, if you screw up, there'll probably be no one there to help. And the consequences of an upset or injury will likely be exponentially more serious.

So try to choose a route that reduces the consequences of an upset. Skip the challenging whitewater. Pick a trip from which you can literally walk away. Once on the river, make your decisions with an eye to conservatism. Portage that drop you might otherwise run. Finally, *make sure someone at home knows your itinerary and when you expect to get home.*

River Signals

One attribute of river safety that is all too infrequently discussed by river runners at the outset of a run is communication. Simply stated, what is the best way to communicate across expanses of water when your party spreads out along the river? Barring the use of walkie-talkies and cell phones, there has to be a way to conduct basic communication on the river. As it turns out, there is, courtesy of the American Whitewater Affiliation.

Described below are some simple river signals that, when reviewed at the start of each trip, can mean the difference between a safe, enjoyable trip and disaster. Commit them to memory and review them at the start of each trip, especially if you are floating with someone new.

You may come across variations of these signals. That's okay. *Make sure,* however, that everyone in your floating group understands and uses the same signals.

Finally, because most of these signals are visual, you need to have a line of sight on at least one other party in your group. Adhere to that rule. If you find yourself getting too far ahead, slow down and wait. If you get too far behind, try to catch up. Here are the basic signals:

Attention. This is an audible signal only. It is a series of short chirps (some recommend a single, long blast) on a whistle. Use this only when other efforts to communicate fail. The other signals need the group's attention to work. Get a good waterproof whistle, and attach it to your vest. You'll be amazed at how often you use it.

Help (emergency signal). Wave a paddle, life jacket, or helmet in a semi-circle over your head while giving three hard blasts on a whistle. Use the visual signals if you have no whistle.

Stop. Hold your paddle horizontally and pump it up and down, or hold your arms straight to the side and flap up and down. Pass the signal back to those behind you.

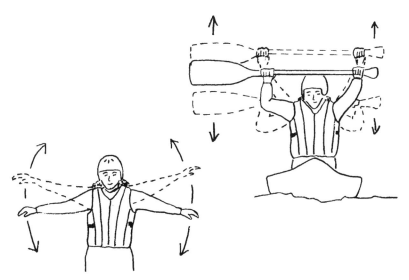

Directions. A paddle held vertically means all clear down the center, or point 45 degrees to the preferred route. *Never* point towards the direction you want people to avoid.

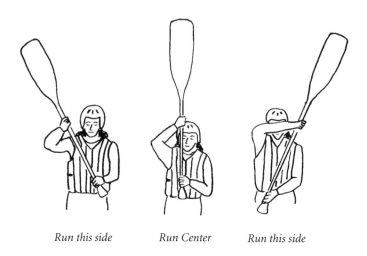

Run this side   *Run Center*   *Run this side*

I'm okay; are you okay? This signal is for notifying your companions that you are all right and to elicit some response back that they are, in turn, okay. It's simple. Just place your hand on top of your head. This is not an AWA signal, but it's a good one to have in your repertoire.

Appendix A
Floater's First-aid Kit

The character of your first-aid kit will change according to whether you are doing a day trip or an extended trip. The longer the trip, and the more isolated you are from medical help, the more extensive your first-aid kit should be.

Important point: Take a first-aid class. The fanciest first-aid kit in the world isn't worth a darn if you don't know how to use it. While the basic American Red Cross course will give you adequate grounding to deal with the most common first-aid problems, there are plenty of good wilderness first-aid courses being taught around the country. Whatever course you decide to take, don't do it just once. The state of the art in first aid is constantly evolving, and an update every couple of years will help you stay abreast of important changes in the field. The other reason to update is that, even where acceptable first-aid practices haven't changed, most of us don't do enough first aid to remember it all. Updates can help overcome rusty skills.

Finally, talk to ten experienced boaters, and you'll hear ten different (sometimes violently so) opinions about what should be in your first-aid kit. What appears below should provide a basic, minimal framework. Tweak it or embellish it according to your own experience or your own violently held opinions.

Personal First-aid Kit—Day Trips

This is the stuff you should carry in your dry bag so that you don't have to constantly chase down the boat that has a bigger kit when all you need is an aspirin or a Band-Aid.

☐ Band-Aids
☐ Neosporin or other disinfectant
☐ Benadryl cream or cortisone cream
☐ Aspirin, ibuprofen, acetaminophen
☐ Sawyer Extractor

☐ Bee sting reducer

☐ Eyeglass repair kit

☐ Anti-diarrhea medicine

☐ Antacid

☐ Sunscreen

☐ Personal prescription medication

Group First-aid Kit

☐ Gauze pads

☐ Duct tape or good adhesive tape

☐ Safety pins

☐ SAM Splint or some other flexible and portable splint material

☐ Triangular bandages

☐ Kling bandages

☐ Scissors

☐ Tweezers

☐ Antihistamines

☐ Stomach stuff (anti-diarrhea, antacid, laxative, etc.)

☐ Needle

☐ Eyeglass repair kit

☐ Notebook and pencil

☐ First-aid manual

Appendix B
Moving Water Rescue Kit

The following is a basic rescue kit, designed to address the most common problems you are likely to encounter on the river. As with your first aid kit, this one won't do you much good if you don't know how to use the tools it contains.

Good knife. There are a number of really good rescue knives on the market. Gerber and Spyderco have both been aggressive about designing good rescue knives for river use, but they are by no means the only options. Talk to your local outdoor shop to see what's available. When you get a rescue knife, use it only for that. Don't use it for slicing cheese or spreading peanut butter or whittling, no matter how tempting the impulse at any given moment. You want it to cut fast when you need it. Also, if the knife is designed for attachment to your vest (most are), make sure it will release easily from your vest when you need it. It won't do you much good if you can't get it off when you need it.

Throw rope (Spectra or Polypro). See Chapter 4, The Basics of River Rescue.

Slings (at least two—four to ten feet long each, of webbing). These are important to provide anchors for your rescue ropes (see Appendix E, Knots and Mechanical Advantage). If they are too short, you won't be able to get them around the likely anchor points (trees, rocks, etc.). So err to the long side when sizing your webbing. Size one of these slings so that it's ready to be used as a seat harness or chest harness.

Prusiks (at least three—two to four feet long each).

Carabiners (at least three) Carabiners have a number of uses. They give you attachment points to boats, they can serve as pulleys in a pinch, or they can allow you to secure gear in your boat. It seems you can never have enough carabiners.

Rescue pulleys (two twist-open pulleys). This is not a place to stint on price. There are some excellent, reasonably priced pulleys, but there are also some really cheap ones that are inadequate. The pulley has to be strong enough to hold against some really heavy loads.

Folding saw. There are a number of really fine backpacking saws on the market. Also, Stanley makes a perfectly good folding saw for about $12 or so that works just fine. What I said about the rescue knife applies here as well. Keep this saw in your rescue kit, and resist the urge to use it for cutting firewood.

Whistle. This should be on your PFD at all times. A pealess one is best, because it will work even when it's wet.

*From left to right, rescue kit items include: **top row** throw bag with polypro rope, throw bag with Spectra rope, waterproof box; **center row,** folding saw, pulleys (below saw), prusiks, slings; **bottom row,** rescue knife, carabiners, whistle.*

Appendix C
The Basic Dry Bag

Regardless of the length of river trip you take—whether a day's float of a few hours on a local river, or a multi-week expedition—there are certain items that you should have close at hand. The following list (annotated with my rationale) reflects my experience. Talk to fifty other experienced river runners, and each of their lists may be a little different. And probably just as valid. But the list below represents my view of what you should have in your daily dry bag (or dry box).

☐ **A source of fire**. This means matches or a lighter in a waterproof container, plus some kind of fire starter. The commercial starters work fine. I normally try to carry three sources of fire with me, in different locations. That way, if one source gets waterlogged, I have a shot at finding some dry matches somewhere else.

☐ **First-aid kit**. See Appendix A.

☐ **Rescue kit**. See Appendix B.

☐ **Spare warm hats**. I have handed warm hats to shivering clients and floating partners innumerable times (it's amazing how often people ignore the hat rule). More than once, those extra hats have rescued people from misery—and in at least one case—serious hypothermia. Keep your eyes peeled for the ugly warm hats on sale, and take some extras; they're cheap and relatively compact—and I guarantee that eventually you'll use them.

☐ **Spare warm gloves or mittens**. See item 4 above. Same deal. Eventually someone won't have these when they really need them.

☐ **Spare thermal socks**. See items 4 and 5 above. These can even double as mittens if necessary. A few years back, on a snowy, blowing fall fishing trip on the Missouri River, one of my fishing buddies had forgotten his gloves. Halfway through the day, his hands were wooden. I offered him mittens, but he opted for my spare socks, which fit him better. His hands warmed up in no time. Those socks were pretty clumsy for tying flies onto his leader, but it was fun to watch him try.

☐ **Spare long underwear tops and bottoms.** Sometimes, after a dunk in the river, the fastest way to warmth is through dry undies.

☐ **Towel.** Dry off before you put on those dry undies.

☐ **Snack food.** See the section on hypothermia in Chapter One, Five Deadly Mistakes.

☐ **Warm jacket.**

☐ **Rain gear**—Skip the ponchos. In a wind, a poncho can be worse than useless.

☐ **Flashlight, spare batteries**—You just never know when you'll need this, but you will.

☐ **Map and compass**—This one is especially important if you're on new water and in new countryside. If you need to get out (or to help) fast, a map of the local area can be invaluable.

☐ **Sunglasses**

☐ **Water bottle (filled)**—Okay, so you probably don't want this in your dry bag. But you definitely want it in the boat. Invaluable protection against dehydration or hypothermia.

☐ **Duct tape**—Truly the universal elixir. Bind wounds. Repair boats. Make a dry suit. Build a house. Build a car. Or a boat.

☐ **Heavy-duty needle and heavy-duty thread or dental floss**— Invaluable as a clothing and raft repair item. With this and duct tape, there's almost nothing you can't fix.

☐ **Cell phones—optional.** I think cell phones, as used by most people—in their cars while driving, in the grocery store, in theaters, etc.—are the work of the devil. I hate them, and if you ever see me driving down the highway with one glued to my ear, shoot me. I'll need to be put out of my misery. But, a growing school of thought recognizes the cell phone as a valuable emergency tool. If you have one, and it will work where you're going, and it gives you additional peace of mind to have it along, then take it. But heed the message of Peter Kummerfeldt, former survival instructor for the U.S. Air Force Academy. Peter has noted the disturbing trend of people relying on their cell phones to get them out of trouble that they should have avoided in the first place. His advice: **Don't let it become a substitute for good judgment.** If you get stupid just because you think the phone provides you with some universal cure-all against the consequences of your actions, you're in for a rude shock. And please, save it for emergencies only. Most of us paddle to get away from the infernal things.

This may seem like a lot of stuff. Maybe it is, but it will fit in a small dry bag without much trouble and it doesn't weigh much. And when you need it, you'll not only be glad you have it, you'll get to wallow in the glow of unfettered smugness, knowing that you're prepared for the worst the weather can dish out. Some of us live for that little glow.

Appendix D
Directory of Schools, Organizations and Other River Safety Resources

I have repeatedly harped on getting training in running rivers—training in how to read rivers, training in how to use your craft, and training in rescue techniques. There are many programs around the country that offer training in river boating. These courses range from public or quasi-public recreational programs at colleges and universities to privately operated paddling schools to nonprofit programs. These programs number in the dozens to hundreds. Below are listed some of the best known. Note: Just because a program isn't well-known doesn't mean it's not any good. Check with your local outdoor shops for a listing of river-safety courses in your area.

College and University Recreational Programs.

Throughout the country, there are many excellent outdoor recreation programs affiliated with colleges and universities. The following list is not exhaustive. Check with your local outdoor shop if you don't see a program near you.

Many of these university programs are open only to students, faculty, and staff. Nonetheless, it's worth checking on what it takes to become a "student." In many cases, it's not terribly hard or expensive to gain student status for the purpose of enjoying a school's recreation program..

Adventure Outings, California State University, Chico
BMU #208 CSUC
Chico, CA 95929
phone: 530-898-4011
fax: 530-898-6359
email: rscott@csuchico.edu
website: www.csuchico/as/adventure
   Adventure Outings offers instruction in the use of rafts, canoes, and kayaks. The training encompasses navigational skills, accident avoidance, and self- and assisted rescue. Courses are open not only to students but also to the general public.

Georgia Institute of Technology
Georgia Tech
750 Ferst Drive
Atlanta, GA 30332-0110
phone: 404-894-6267
fax: 404-894-8894
website: www.cyberbuzz.gatech.edu/orgt

Georgia Tech offers rafting, canoeing, and kayaking with an emphasis on whitewater. They offer courses from beginner to expert, and cover basic river safety in all of them.

Georgia State University
Recreational Services—Touch the Earth Program
University Plaza
Atlanta, GA 30303
phone: 404-651-3634
fax: 404-651-1190
website: www.gsu.edu/~wwwrec/touch

This program has been around since 1974 and offers whitewater canoe and kayak clinics as well as whitewater rafting trips. All are instructional and supervised by whitewater leaders. The program offers river rescue training for its leaders and guides. The instruction involves not only navigational, accident avoidance, and river skills, but also safety training. The courses are geared toward "never-ever" beginners. There is a heavy emphasis on training and supervision in all courses. The courses are offered to GSU students, faculty, and staff and their guests first and then, in a limited way, to non-university persons. Students not enrolled in the university pay more than those in the university community.

Idaho State University Outdoor Program
P.O. Box 8128
Pocatello, ID 83209
phone: 208-236-3912
fax: 208-236-4600
email: walkpete@isu.edu
website: www.isu.edu/outdoor

ISU offers semester-long classes in kayaking to enrolled students, and three- to five-day workshops on rafting, canoeing, kayaking, and river rescue. All the classes include some training in and discussion of basic safety considerations, while the river rescue course is much more detailed and involves more hands-on practice. All classes cover river reading, navigation, accident avoidance, self-rescue, assisted rescue, and a discussion of safety equipment and its proper use. Classes are open to the general public as well as to students, faculty, and staff.

Middle Tennessee State University
Outdoor Pursuits
Campus Recreation
Box 556
Murfreesboro, TN 37037
phone: 615-698-2104
fax: 615-898-5568
website: www.mtsu.edu/camprec
    MTSU's program includes workshops in reading whitewater, kayak roll workshops, and whitewater trips that entail instruction in basic boating skills (canoe, raft, and kayak), safety, identification of hazards, scouting hazards, and self- and assisted rescue. The program is geared to the university community.

Paul Smith's College
College Outdoor Center
Paul Smith's, NY 12970
phone: 518-327-6389
fax: 518-327-6161
email: tuckerj@paulsmiths.edu
    Paul Smith's program includes introductory kayaking with an emphasis on skills training, river reading, accident avoidance, and self- and assisted rescue. The program is available to students, faculty, and staff.

St. Lawrence University
Canton, NY 13617
phone: 315-229-5377
fax: 315-229-5709
email: pry@music.stlawu.edu
    St. Lawrence offers one, two, and five-day courses in whitewater kayaking and canoeing, as well as a strong wilderness tripping program. All the courses stress river rescue (self- and assisted), reading the water, recognizing river classification, river geomorphology, personal safety, group safety, accident avoidance, leading a group on moving water, and techniques and equipment. The instructors make a "concerted effort to teach people to match their level of ability with the appropriate river." The wilderness tripping course addresses the special safety issues of wilderness boating. The courses are offered to students, faculty, and staff.

San Juan College
Outdoor Leadership and Recreation Programs
4601 College Blvd
Farmington, NM 87402
phone: 505-599-0487
fax: 505-599-0385
email: moskowitz@sjc.cc.nm.ux

website: www.sjc.cc.nm.ux

The San Juan College program offers a certification in outdoor leadership, which includes training in rafting and swift-water rescue. As of August 1999, a canoe class was on the near horizon. This training includes work on self-rescue, throw bags, boat flips, wrapped boats, etc., in addition to basic rafting techniques, rigging, river reading, and raft repair. The courses are available only to San Juan College students, but it is easy to enroll and there is only a $15 per credit-hour fee.

Touch the Earth Outdoor Recreation and Education
MacBride Nature Recreation Area
University of Iowa, Division of Recreational Services
E216 Field House
Iowa City, IA 52242-1111
phone: 319-335-9290
email: wayne-fett@uiowa.edu

This program has a whitewater canoeing and kayaking program. The program offers basic safety training which includes river reading, navigational skills, accident avoidance, self- and assisted rescue. The program is open to students, faculty, staff, and the general public.

UCLA Outdoor Adventures
2131 John Wooden Center
Los Angeles, CA 90095-1612
phone: 310-206-1252
fax: 310-825-6321
email: sreynolds@saonet.ucla.edu
website: www.saonet.ucla.edu/recreate/

UCLA offers training in river reading, navigational skills, accident avoidance, self- and assisted rescue for canoeing and kayaking. The training includes discussion, demonstration, and practice of basic safety techniques. The courses are available to student, faculty, staff, and alumni association members.

University of Alberta Paddling Society
Student Union, Box 132
University of Alberta
Edmonton, AB, Canada T6G 2J7
phone: 403-492-2767
fax: 403-492-1881
email: jhutchis @per.ualberta.ca
website: www.ualberta.ca

The UAPS is open to both students and non-students for a modest fee. The club offers beginner to advanced kayak lessons. The introductory "theory sessions" involve a discussion of river safety, and the club includes on-river safety sessions during the summer.

University of Calgary Outdoor Program Centre
2500 University Drive NW
Calgary, AB, Canada T2N 1N4
phone: 403-220-6800
fax: 403-284-5867
email: askrasti@ucalgary.ca
website: www.ucalgary.ca/opc

This program offers basic and advanced river safety and skills instruction in kayaking, canoeing, and rafting. It also offers a whitewater rescue course and a kayak instructor certification course. Its course runs the gamut from basic to advanced in river reading, navigation, accident avoidance, and various rescue techniques. All the courses are open to the general public.

University of California, Berkeley
5 Haas Clubhouse SCRA
Berkeley, CA 94720
phone: 510-642-4000
fax: 510-642-8556
website: www.strawberry.org/caladv/rafting.html

UC Berkeley offers whitewater raft trips and a week-long guide training school. The guide training school, directed at training whitewater rafting guides, focuses on river hydrology, paddling technique, boat control, river safety, rescue, teamwork, and leadership. No previous rafting experience is necessary to take this course.

University of Utah Department of Parks, Recreation, and Tourism Natural Resources Learning Courses
250 S 1850 East, Rm 200
Salt Lake City, UT 84112-0920
phone: 801-585-3204
fax: 801-581-4930
email: John.Cederquist@health.utah.edu

Water-based courses with enrollment open to all persons include river running, river rescue, canoeing, kayaking, rafting, sailing, and fishing. These classes are offered for credit, or may be taken non-credit. Most involve two nights of classroom instruction and an absorbing weekend at one of Utah's scenic outdoor settings. Many ability levels are accommodated. Students learn outdoor recreation skills and behaviors, explore natural resource management and policy issues, develop leadership ability, and enrich social interactions.

Private Paddling Schools.

Many of the private paddling schools emphasize training in specific paddle craft, especially canoes and kayaks. Be sure that you inquire as to the kind of training offered. The schools described are by no means the only possible choices. The leading paddle magazines list canoe and kayak programs all over the country. In addition, whitewater guide schools, such as those listed below, while a little more pricey than some of the more basic courses (typically in the range of $300 to $800), are an excellent source of basic skills training.

American River Recreation
P.O. Box 465
Lotus, CA 95651
phone: 530-622-6802
fax: 530-622-2512
email: info@arrafting.com
website: www.arrafting.com
   This school offers 8-day rafting courses that cover all areas of whitewater rafting and related skills, including basic safety and rescue techniques. It is designed to not only train guides but to enhance the skills of the private boater.

Mad River Boat Trips Guide School
1255 S. Hwy 89
P.O. Box 10940
Jackson, WY 83002
phone: 800-458-7238
fax: 307-733-6203
email: info@mad-river.com
website: www.mad-river.com
   This program provides participants with training in all aspects of whitewater rafting, covering everything from knots to boat care, to rowing, and river rescue. Part of the course emphasis is to train people to guide trips on the Snake River.

Nantahala Outdoor Center
13077 Hwy 19 West
Bryson City, NC 28713-9114
phone: 1-828-488-2176
fax: 828-488-2498
email: johel@noc.com

website: www.nocweb.com

In business since 1972, Nantahala is probably the oldest and most renowned of the paddling schools in the United States. Its curriculum includes every kind of river running program imaginable, from basic canoe, kayaking, or rafting techniques to advanced whitewater training to swift-water rescue. In addition, for those with some boating experience it includes guide training courses that provide intensive instruction in basic safety and rescue techniques, and trip planning.

Rocky Mountain Outdoor Center
10281 Hwy 50
Howard, CO 81233
phone: 1-800-255-5784
website: www.adventuresports.com

Rocky Mountain Outdoor Center offers everything from canoe and kayak courses to rescue courses to a two-week whitewater guide school. The guide school, designed to prepare its students to meet the Colorado requirements for for guiding, offers comprehensive training in equipment, raft rigging, river reading, boat handling, safety orientation, trip organization, and rescue.

National Outdoor Leadership School
288 Main St
Lander, WY 82520
phone: 307-332-5300
fax: 307-332-1220
email: admissions@nols.edu
website: www.nols.edu

NOLS is one of the best known outdoor leadership schools in North America. While NOLS is not a paddling school per se (their course offerings include everything from mountain climbing to winter camping instruction), they offer courses that include whitewater paddling.

Outward Bound
RT 9D R2 Box 280
Garrison, NY 10524
phone: 914-424-4000
fax: 914-424-4121
email: 73762.1351@compuserve.com
website: www.outwardbound.com

Outward Bound is one of the oldest outdoor leadership schools in North America, with school locations throughout the United States. A number of the courses are water based, including canoe-based courses in Minnesota and raft-based courses in Colorado.

Whitewater Voyages
Whitewater Guide School
5225 San Pablo Dam Road
El Sobrante, CA 94803-3309
phone: 800-488-7238
fax: 510-758-7238
email: schools@whitewatervoyages.com
website: www.whitewatervoyages.com
    Whitewater Voyages offers seven-day guide training courses for both fixed-oar craft and paddle boats. The course includes intensive workshops on reading the water, boat handling, river safety, and advanced rescue techniques and procedures.

River Safety Programs and Rescue Courses

American Canoe Association
7432 Alban Station Blvd
Springfield, VA 22150
phone: 703-451-0141
    ACA sponsors extensive training in both canoe and kayak skills. These courses range from beginning to advanced technique. In addition, ACA offers a two-day river rescue course. ACA programs are available all over the United States.

American Red Cross
17th and D Street
Washington, DC 20006
phone: 202-728-6400
    ARC over the years has offered excellent paddling courses for canoe and kayak with a heavy emphasis on safety. In addition, they offer excellent training in cardiopulmonary resuscitation (CPR) and basic first aid.

American Whitewater Affiliation
PO Box 85
Phoenicia, NY 12646
phone: 914-688-5569
website: www.awa.org
    Don't let the "whitewater" in the name put you off. AWA has been a leader in river safety over the years, having developed a widely recognized safety code (most of which is incorporated into this book in one fashion or another). The AWA website includes the AWA River Safety Code and an analysis of whitewater accidents.

Rescue 3 International
PO Box 519
Elk Grove, CA 95759-0519
phone: 1-800-457-3728

Rescue 3 offers an exceptional river-rescue program. The Swiftwater Rescue Technician Course is a thirty-plus hour course that incorporates a lot of hands-on practical instruction. Rescue 3 sponsors courses all over the United States and has been the template for a number of other rescue courses.

Princeton University Outdoor Action
"Planning a Safe River Trip," by Rick Curtis
website: www.trakkerinc.com/trans/trsafer.htm

This entry could as well go in the bibliography. This website has an excellent discussion of planning a safe river trip, with checklists, discussions of hazards, and formulas for reducing the likelihood of having an accident on a river trip.

Peter Kummerfeldt
6612 Frederick Drive
Colorado Springs, CO 80918
phone: 719-593-5852
email: peterk@outdoorsafe.com
website: www.outdoorsafe.com

While Peter doesn't focus on watersports in his offerings, he is a walking, talking encyclopedia of outdoor survival. His website is chock full of good information on how to keep yourself out of trouble in the outdoors, and has a lot of information that translates well into time spent on rivers.

Appendix E
Knots and Mechanical Advantage

While there are a myriad of knots that are valuable for the floater to know, this appendix will cover only a few of them—specifically, those knots valuable to issues of safety and rescue. There are a number of really good knot books on the market. See the Bibliography for at least one of these.

As discussed in Chapter Four, The Basics of River Rescue, fast is best. If you have to pull a boat off a rock with a rope and you can do it by simply attaching the rope and tugging, good for you. Do it. Sometimes, though, the boat is really stuck, and all the brute force and ignorance that you can muster on a straight line to the boat aren't enough. In those moments, you need some mechanical advantage.

The riggings described here are wonderfully simple to do. Like all the other stuff I've discussed in this book, however, if you don't practice them, you won't be able to do them when you need them. These riggings are just the tip of the iceberg in mechanical possibilities. There is a universe of other options beyond those described here. A good rescue course will put your average pathological knot freak in hog heaven with pig riggings, Tyrolean traverses, two-point self-equalizing anchors, and the like. In the meantime, what you see here will cover most of what you're likely to need.

Knots

First, to make these mechanical advantages work, you need to know a few basic knots:

Water Knot for a Web Sling

This is the knot you use to make a sling out of the webbing in your rescue kit. Give yourself a fair amount of extra sling as you tie this knot, because you will get some slippage when you first tighten it. Once you have the knot formed, snug it down until it stops slipping.

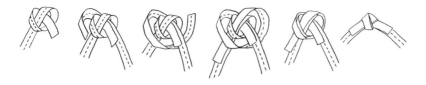

Double Overhand

Use this knot on one-quarter-inch kernmantle line to make prussic loops.

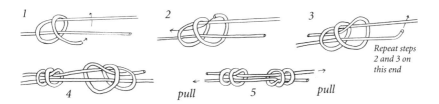

Repeat steps 2 and 3 on this end

pull   *pull*

Three-Wrap Prusik

When a prusik is applied to another line, it will bind on that line and not slip when force is applied to the loop. When you remove the tension from the loop, it will easily loosen and move. This knot is crucial to setting up a Z-drag.

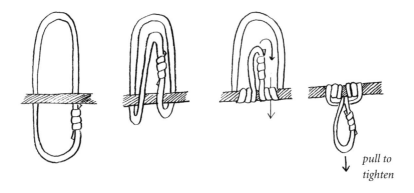

pull to tighten

Figure-8 on a Bight

Use this one to attach your line to the boat. A number of rescue experts now recommend this knot over a bowline for hauling on a heavy load because it's stronger and easier to tie.

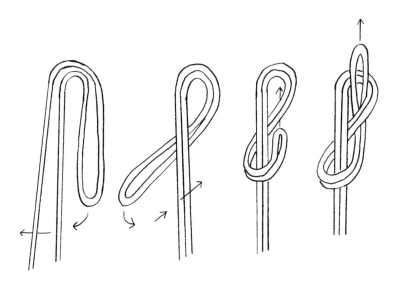

Bowline

This is a good one for tying on painters or flip lines. You can reef on it all day long and it's still easy to untie.

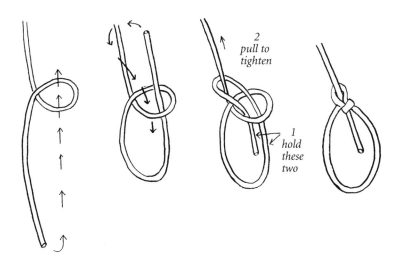

Trucker's Hitch

Great knot for tying things—boats to the tops of cars, loads into boats—down tight. Once you know this knot, you'll wonder how you ever got along without it.

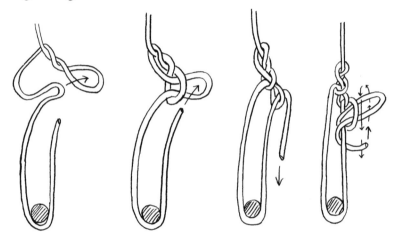

The No-Knot

This is a handy trick for those times when you don't have a web sling to anchor your line. It is also good for tethering your boat to shore. It relies on friction to hold the line in place.

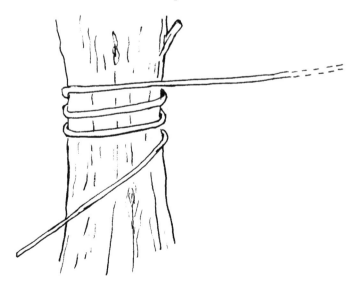

Gaining Mechanical Advantage

One-to-One Leverage

If you pull on an object in a straight line, the amount of force you apply to your end of the rope translates into the same amount of force at the boat (1:1). If you apply fifty pounds of force at your end of the rope, you will get fifty pounds at the boat.

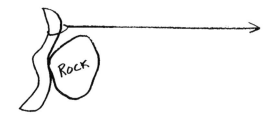

Likewise, if you pull through a pulley attached to the shore—while you may be able to change the direction of your pull—you gain no mechanical advantage. Fifty pounds on your end gets you fifty pounds at the boat (1:1).

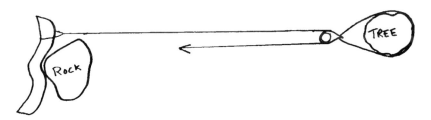

Two-to-One Leverage

The simplest leverage you can get is a two-to-one (2:1) ratio by attaching the rope to an anchor on shore, and running the rope through a pulley on the boat. With this system, fifty pounds of force on your end of the rope yields one hundred pounds of force at the boat.

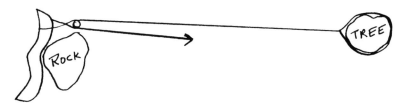

Three-to-One Leverage
(The Z-Drag)

The Z-drag is a relatively simple, really neat way to generate a leverage of 3:1. It involves using two pulleys to increase the leverage. Neither pulley attaches to the boat, however. To do this rig, you'll need—besides your rescue rope and anchor sling—two pulleys (carabiners, while not as good, will work in place of the pulleys) and two prusik loops. Here's what it looks like:

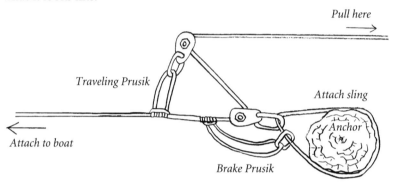

Pull here

Traveling Prusik

Attach sling

Anchor

Attach to boat

Brake Prusik

Once you have this set up, try pulling on it against a load—even a load of just a few pounds. You'll notice that the pulley away from the anchor (the moving pulley) will soon be right up against the anchor pulley. So you have to slide the moving pulley back down the rope toward the boat. The prusik sling at the anchor is important to keep you from losing ground when you have to make that move. If you have help, it's important to have someone attend to the anchor prusik so that it doesn't get pulled into the anchor pulley.

Appendix F
River Etiquette

At first glance, this may seem like an inappropriate topic for a book on river safety. Just the contrary is true. By the time you get this far into the book, it's pretty clear that awareness is key to river safety—awareness of the river features, awareness of your own limitations, and awareness of other people on the river. Etiquette on the river is the logical extension of that awareness. The rules below are grounded in one thing—respect. If you have respect for others on the river and near it, you probably don't have to read these rules. You probably already adhere to them. If you don't give a hoot for anyone else on the river, then reading these rules won't change your mind, and sooner or later you'll run into somebody who'll be happy to club these rules into your thick head. On the other hand, if you're just getting started, consider these as rules of the road—guideposts to behavior that, at the very least, will reduce conflict and needless irritation.

• **Don't hog the launch area.** Most public launching areas have some point at which to launch your boat—either a ramp or an open place on the shore. There is nothing more irritating than having to sit and cool your heels while some nitwits unpack their gear, inflate their boats, repack their food, and generally hold things up. Don't do it to others, unpack your stuff away from the boat ramp so that others can launch their boats while you're getting ready.

• **If you get to a put-in and it's full to overflowing, consider going somewhere else.** A lot of put-ins have a specific limit as to how many vehicles it can handle. Usually, the parking slops out on to public roadways, creating a hazard for anyone driving by or getting out of the car; or it slops onto private land, creating a completely different set of problems.

• **On the river, don't crowd other boats.** This should be a cardinal rule, and violation of it should result in swift and brutal punishment—a lifetime sentence to porta-potty duty, or twenty-four hours straight of irritating music to be chosen by the victim of your crowding—something along those lines, anyway. Crowding is not only extremely annoying, but in the wrong water, it can be out-and-out dangerous. There may be no more helpless feeling than being pushed out of your line at the top of a rapid by some slack-jaw in a bigger craft than you.

• **If you're on a fishing river, try to give anglers—especially those wading— as much room as you can.** Again there's the irritation factor. But a wading angler is especially vulnerable to people coming down current in boats. Avoiding mishaps here is a two part chore—first, anticipating what's ahead, and second, showing a little respect for the other person's recreation. As you approach an angler, try to see where she is fishing, and try to avoid going into that water. A lot of times, if an angler is well in the current, you might be able to go behind her and completely avoid trashing the water she is fishing. If you have no recourse but to go through the water she is fishing, apologize, and try to get through as quickly as you can. It's amazing how far a well-placed apology can go toward soothing ruffled feathers. In either case, let the angler know you are there and what your intentions are before you get there. If you're the wading angler and you get floaters who simply can't avoid your water despite their best efforts, cut them some slack, and at least appreciate their effort.

• **If you are playing on a rapid or at some other spot on the river, pay attention to boats coming through the rapid and yield to the through traffic.** This should be a no-brainer.

• **If you bring your dog along, keep it under control. If you can't control it, leave it home.** It's not amusing to have some strange dog come lumbering into your lunch spot, snuffling in your food packs and crapping in the picnic area. So don't inflict that kind of intrusion on others with your dog.

• **Try to keep the size of your group from getting too large.** This goes to a basic safety issue. If a group is too large, it is difficult to keep track of people, and scouting can become difficult and excessively time-consuming. If you have a large group, consider breaking into a number of smaller groups and putting some separation on the river between them.

• **Try to keep the decibel level down to something less than a dull roar.** Most floaters aren't there just for the unbridled pleasure of listening to your favorite boom-box tunes or to hear your group discussion from hundreds of yards away. And if your tunes are so precious to you that you can't go on the river without your boom box, stay off the river.

• **Respect the rights of adjoining landowners.** While you may well enjoy a public easement to float the river through private lands (not necessarily so in all states), that right usually ends above the ordinary high-water mark. Know the limits of your rights and abide by them.

• **Avoid behavior that damages the natural resource associated with the river.** Don't litter. Don't gratuitously shoot everything, animate or inanimate, that you encounter. Don't drag your anchor (if you have one), along the bottom of the river. And don't take your ax to the trees or decide to cut a custom log table, or otherwise trash the streamside vegetation. Leave any rocks or historic artifacts where you find them.

Respect any wildlife you encounter. Don't harass animals and don't feed them. If you see animals nesting or mating, don't go up and butt in on them. Leave them alone.

• **If you're camping, try to use established campsites, and, in any event, practice no-trace camping.** Don't alter a site to create a campsite. Focus your activities in areas of minimal vegetation. Don't build a fire if you don't really need one. If you do need a fire, try to leave no trace of it behind. Use a fire pan if you can.

• **Dispose of wastes properly.** Use public toilets or latrines where they exist. When you can't use a public toilet (and sometimes you just can't wait) pack out any solid wastes or dig a cat hole 6 to 8 inches deep at least 200 feet from water. If you do a cat hole, cover and disguise it when you're done. In areas of heavy use, the cat hole option is simply not good enough. Pack out anything that you have packed in. If you're washing dishes, carry water 200 feet away from streams or lakes and use small amounts of biodegradable soap. Scatter strained dishwater.

• **Know the regulations and special concerns for the areas you visit.** If a river has specific regulations, honor them. They will usually address some specific problem. Don't become part of the problem by flouting the regulations.

APPENDIX G
MISCELLANEOUS HAZARDS

The main focus of this book is on the hazards and challenges that you find between the ordinary high water marks—river features, navigation problems, and your own mindset. There are a number of other factors that might adversely affect your well-being on the river that are not confined to the banks of the river. These are things that can occur on any river on the continent.

Weather

Lightning. Lightning storms can come out of nowhere quickly. If you see a storm coming, get off the river and wait for it to pass. Try to stay off prominent terrain features like hilltops or ridges, metal structures, shallow caves or overhangs (ground currents can arc across these) and away from prominent, solitary trees. A flat with low lying willows is as good a place as any. But, even if your bankside options aren't great, they're all better than staying on the river. Once on the bank, don't huddle together. Spread out. If all you have is open, grassy bank, get as low as you can with your feet close together, and put down any items that might serve as conductors (graphite fishing rods, carbon fiber oars, etc.).

Wind. Most commonly regarded as a lake hazard, river winds can be just as dangerous. The Wild and Scenic stretch of the Missouri in Montana, a classic flat water river, has been the scene of more than one wind-aided drowning. When the wind makes navigation difficult, get off the river and wait it out. Also, see Chapter Three, Navigation.

Heavy Rains. Heavy rains can raise the level of a river alarmingly fast. As the river rises, its character changes. In the arid West, this sudden change can present itself as a flash flood. If you get caught in a deluge and you can see the river start to rise, get off. Wait and see if it levels out.

If it doesn't stabilize, stay off.

Pick a spot to get out that allows you to retreat to higher ground if you have to. Pulling off on a gravel bar at the base of a cliff may be no better than staying in the river. Also, don't hunker down in the mouth of a gully. There's a reason it's a gully, and if you try to sit out a gully-washer in one, you may just become an unwilling washee. And make sure you tie your boat to something solid on shore.

Heat. This is the flip-side of hypothermia. It is indeed possible to suffer heat exhaustion or, worse, heat stroke, surrounded by water. The key to avoiding this hazard, common in midsummer, is to layer properly (light colored, breathable cottons), and drink lots of fluids. If it gets too hot, paddle on either end of the day, and get off the river and out of the sun during the worst of the heat.

Sunburn. This should be obvious. Apply sunscreen regularly. Wear clothes that cover your skin. Wear a hat. And if you're going to wear those cool-looking river sandals, sunscreen every bit of bare foot.

CRITTERS

Stinging bugs. Stinging bugs—bees, wasps, hornets, spiders, scorpions—are everywhere. Look out for them, and carry a Sawyer Extractor, and one of the sting reducers. If anyone in your group is allergic to bug bites, make sure you know that ahead of time and carry an insect bite kit. If you're the one with the allergic reactions to bug bites, you should carry an insect bite kit and alert your trip companions about your allergy and the location of your kit.

Snakes. Snakes, poisonous or otherwise, generally want to avoid you as much as you do them. If you're in snake country, watch where you are walking. That may sound obvious, but it's easily forgotten in the distraction of the trip. Oh, and snakes can swim. If you're in the middle of the river with a swimming snake, your boat may look like the next best thing to dry land. Just row or paddle away from it. Whacking it with your paddle probably is just going to make it mad. Besides, it shouldn't have to die just because it scared the crap out of you.

Ticks. In this age of Lyme disease and Rocky Mountain Spotted Fever, if you find a tick attached to you, note the date, and mention it to your doctor it if you later fall ill. Insect repellents may help reduce tick bites.

Other biting insects. Mosquitoes, black flies, deer flies, horse flies, chiggers, and sand fleas are the most ubiquitous and most annoying of the menagerie. Use repellent, cover exposed skin, use a bug jacket if appropriate, and close off shirt and pant cuffs. If the bugs are going to be really bad—giving you an arm-clawing, gibbering case of hysterics—time your trip for periods of light bug activity. In most places this is late spring, late summer, and fall. As to insect repellents be careful in choosing one for children, because they may be more sensitive to the active ingredients. For example, avoid using repellents on children that have more than 35 percent DEET. Also, don't apply repellents too frequently or to irritated skin.

RIVER SAFETY BIBLIOGRAPHY

This bibliography contains both books and videos. This is not an exhaustive list, but it covers some of the best stuff. Make it a habit to pay attention to what is new in the instructional book and video market. There is a lot of good stuff continually coming out. Read and watch as much of it as you can. That said, the same caution applies here as elsewhere—while the resources below are worthwhile learning aids, they are not, by themselves, sufficient to teach you all that you need to know. Get some hands-on instruction and experience.

Cold, Wet, and Alive. Video. Springfield, Virginia: American Canoe Association, 1989. This video offers a good discussion of the causes and treatment of hypothermia.

The Drowning Machine. Video. State College, Pennsylvania: Film Space, Inc., 1980. Watch this video and have the pants scared off you. If you ever thought that running a low-head dam was a neat idea, this video should cure you of any such foolishness.

Bechdel, Les, and Slim Say. *River Rescue.* 2d Ed. Boston: Appalachian Mountain Club, 1989. One of the bibles of river rescue.

Ford, Kent. *Whitewater Self-Defense.* Video. Durango, Colorado: Performance Video and Instruction, 1998. While this video focuses on whitewater kayaking, its discussion of preventing accidents—and how to quickly respond to them—is valuable for any boater.

Ford, Kent, and Les Bechdel. *River Rescue.* Video. Jersey City, New Jersey: Gravity Sports Films. The video based on the book. Excellent depiction of rescue techniques.

Gullion, Laurie. *American Canoe Association Instructor's Manual.* Springfield, Virginia: American Canoe Association, 1987. While this manual is oriented to canoeing, it has a good, concise discussion of the five deadly mistakes.

Heads Up! River Rescue for River Runners. Video. Springfield, Virginia: American Canoe Association, 1993. This video does a great job of showing quick and practical rescue techniques for the average river runner. Buy this video, and look at it over and over. There's more here than you can absorb in one viewing.

McKown, Doug. *Canoeing Safety and Rescue.* Calgary, Alberta: Rocky Mountain Books, 1992. Good discussion of basic safety and rescue techniques.

Schimelpfenig, Todd, and Linda Lindsey. *NOLS Wilderness First Aid.* Lander, Wyoming, 1991. While this title focuses on wilderness first aid, it is an excellent reference for anyone who spends a lot of time outdoors.

Small Craft Safety. St. Louis, Missouri: American Red Cross, 1998. This is a workbook for the American Red Cross Small Craft Safety Program. While it covers small boats in general on all types of waters, it has some good concise discussions of moving water safety issues, including safety and rescue.

Streeks, Neale. *Drift Boat Strategies; Rowing and Fishing Skills for the Western Angler.* Boulder, Colorado: Pruett Publishing, 1997. Don't be put off by the title in this book. While it looks heavily at float fishing, it has an excellent section on basic rowing skills that would be applicable to all river rowing.

Walbridge, Charles. *Knots for Paddlers. Birmingham, Alabama:* Menasha Ridge Press, 1995. Everybody needs knots. This book pretty well covers the gamut.

Walbridge, Charles. *River Safety Anthology.* Springfield, Virginia: American Canoe Association, 1996. While directed at experienced paddlers, these accounts of whitewater accidents are compelling reading and highly instructive for everyone.

Walbridge, Charles. *The American Canoe Association River Safety Reports.* Springfield, Virginia: American Canoe Association, 1982–1985, 1986–1988, 1989–1991, 1992–1996. More accident reports from Walbridge.

Walbridge, Charles, and Wayne A. Sundmacher. *Whitewater Rescue Manual.* Camden, Maine: Ragged Mountain Press, 1995. An excellent discussion of whitewater rescue, bolstered with lots of firsthand accounts of actual rescues. Really readable. While oriented to whitewater rescue, there is a lot of good stuff in here for the casual paddler.

Index

ABOUT THE AUTHOR

A backslid lawyer, Stan Bradshaw has more than twenty-five years of river floating experience, has taught canoeing for eleven years, and is certified by the American Canoe Association for flat,  moving, and whitewater instruction. In his former life as a lawyer, he spent many years working for Montana Trout Unlimited, the cold-water fisheries conservation organization, on stream access, water quality, and instream flow issues. He remains active in environmental and access issues, and still finds time to fly fish, guide anglers, and publish books.